A Life Story
In 50 Christmas Cards
1945-2003

A Life Story
In 50 Christmas Cards
1945-2003

WARREN ROY

BAYEUX

Library and Archives Canada Cataloguing in Publication Data

Roy, Warren, 1929 –
A Life Story in 50 Christmas Cards, 1945 – 2003 / Warren Roy

Includes bibliographical references
ISBN 1-896209-85-8

1. Roy, Warren S., 1929-. 2. Christmas cards. I. Title

NC1868.R69A4 2006 741.971 C2006-901885-5

Published by
Bayeux Arts, Inc.
119 Stratton Crescent SW
Calgary, Canada T3H 1T7
www.bayeux.com

Printed in Canada by
grafikom. Calgary

The publisher gratefully acknowledges the financial support of the Canada Council for the Arts, the Alberta Foundation for the Arts, and the Government of Canada through the Book Publishing Industry Development Program.

To my wife, Heidi, whose constant encouragement and persuasion were the sparks that kept me producing at least a modest amount of art work each year, including these Christmas cards.

CONTENTS

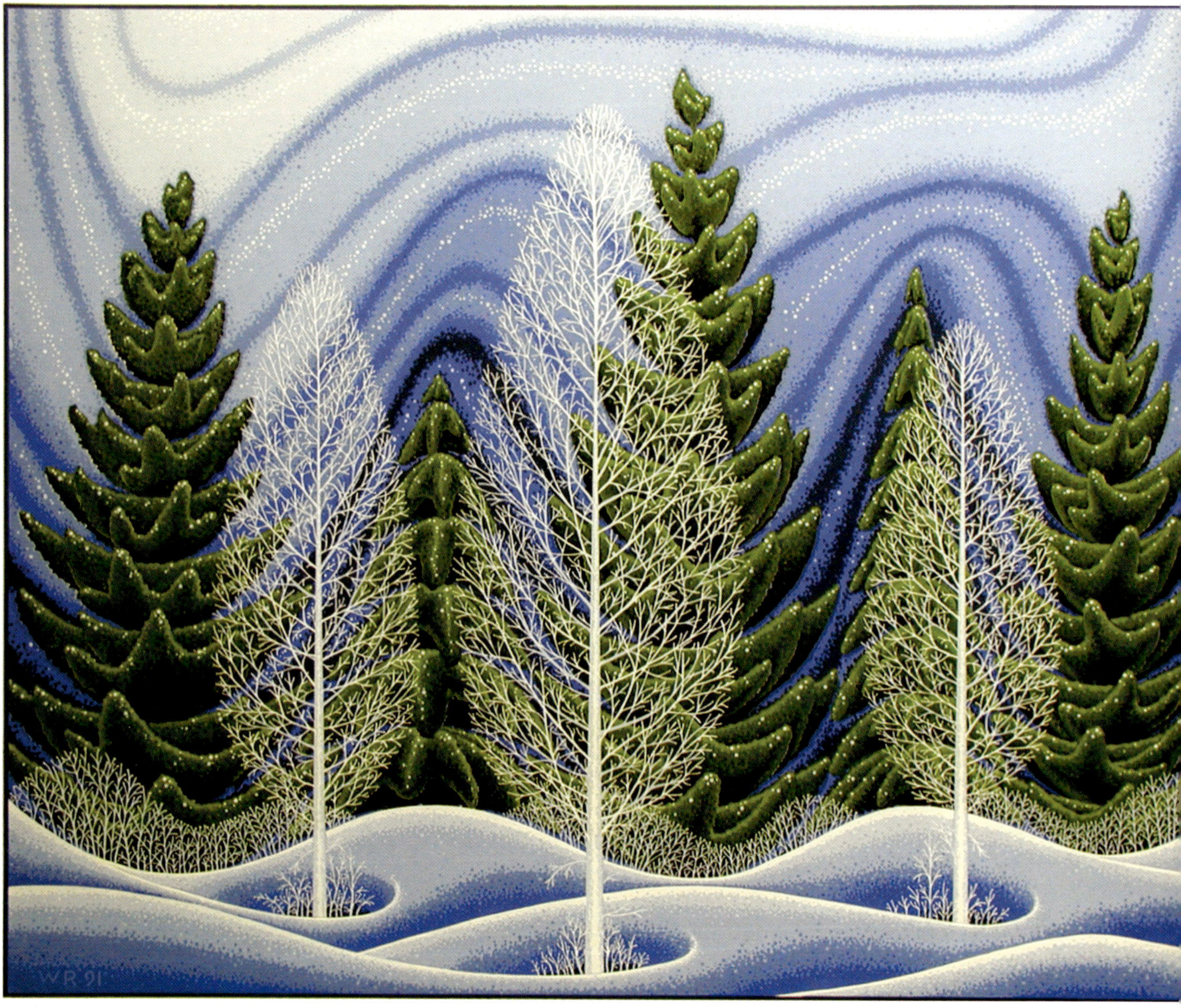

Hoarfrost 1991, serigraph, 43 x 53 cm

PPREFACE

With solid encouragement from my wife, Heidi, and other family members and friends, and with Heidi's continuous organizational and editorial help, this little book of original Christmas cards has come into being.

Why publish a book of fifty "homemade" Christmas cards? One reason is that sending holiday greeting cards through the mail is, sadly, a fast disappearing custom. Hectic time schedules and the increasing use of e-mail are the main reasons for the demise of this old, admittedly time-consuming, but warmly human tradition. This small volume recalls those years when nearly all Canadians exchanged greeting cards at Christmas time. The fifty cards in this book were designed over a period of fifty-eight years and will, I hope, give the reader a glimpse into how the life of a family and the shape of society have changed over the six decades.

The greeting card, whether commercially produced or an original creation of the sender, will never be considered a major art form. In this book there is no editing or selection of the fifty cards reproduced. My very first card, made when I was sixteen, is included with all its flaws. With the passing years, as I gradually formed the personal "custom" of making my own card (nearly) every year, the quality of the work varied, of course, but the topics chosen were usually pertinent to the era or to the lives of my family or me. All cards that were produced, regardless of merit, have been included with no omissions!

Designing, producing and sending about 150 Christmas cards each year was becoming a tall order for Heidi and me, so we agreed, reluctantly, to terminate the practice after I designed my fiftieth card. Now, we have spent the time accrued in producing this book, that we hope will interest people who can appreciate the work of a "Sunday painter", which in a modest way, marks the end of an era.

Warren Roy

MIXED MEDIA ART

In addition to the Christmas cards in this volume, I have included reproductions of three other pieces in various media—to help tell my story:

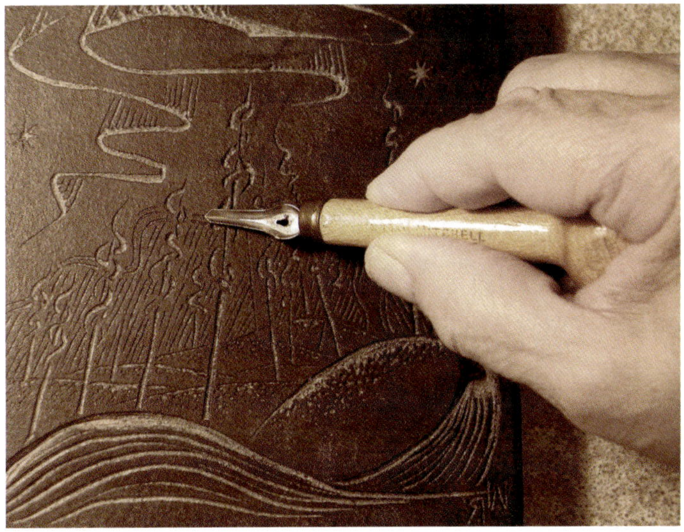

: first eleven Christmas cards, pp 12 to 33, are ɔ**cuts**. A simple, strong graphic technique, the linocut ;eldom used these days. The process involved the ıd carving of a printing block with special chisels. : block was made of a material the same as or similar he thick "battleship linoleum" used in the hallways ɔublic buildings back then. I was usually able to rent use of a platen press in local printing houses, but if essary, a lino block could be hand printed with an roller and the back of a spoon to press the paper to inked block! On one occasion I remember using the ringer" on an old-fashioned washing machine to ss the paper to the block. It was simply a matter of sing the inked block and the paper through the rollers he wringer.

: degree of success in these early cards varied considerably from year to year. Early instruction and guidance m my art teacher, the late Ernest Lindner, in grade 11 and 12 had the strongest and most lasting effect on all of art work, including linocuts. Mr. Lindner always stressed the importance of staying within the discipline of medium and respecting the inherent limitations imposed. In this way, he explained, your work takes on a unity l harmony involving all elements of your design. The linocut is a medium best suited for broad, simple shapes l lines, but quite intricate textures may be achieved.

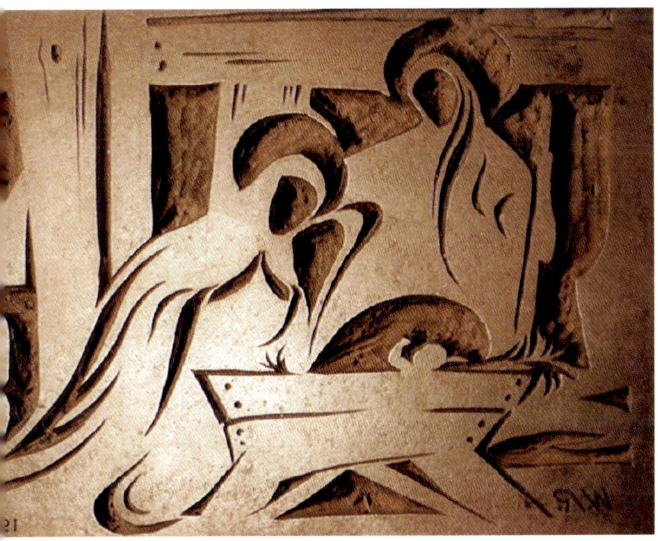

The Original Lino Block

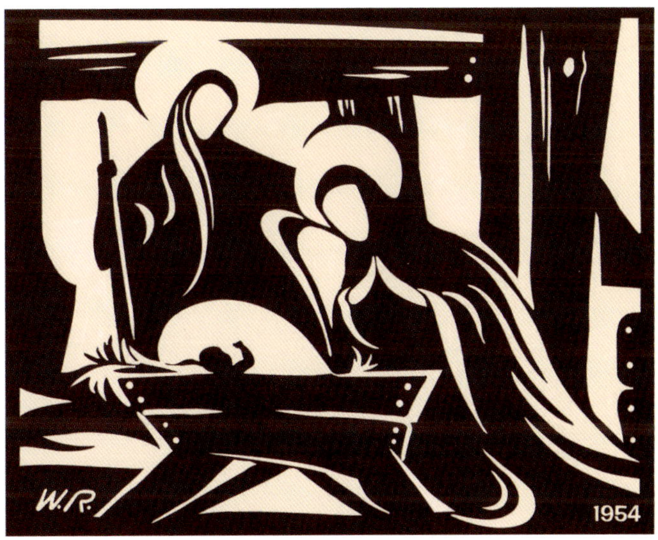

The Print (See p 23.)

FARM HOME
1945

On a farm in Saskatchewan, a boy of sixteen, taking art and other grade 10 subjects by correspondence, I made this, my first linocut Christmas card. Of course the style and the technique are both very much at the beginner's stage. Also, it would seem that my concept of what a "Christmas card" should be was somewhat naïve, but probably quite sincere: Christmas cards must have either holly or poinsettias, some snow, and perhaps a few stars or candles!

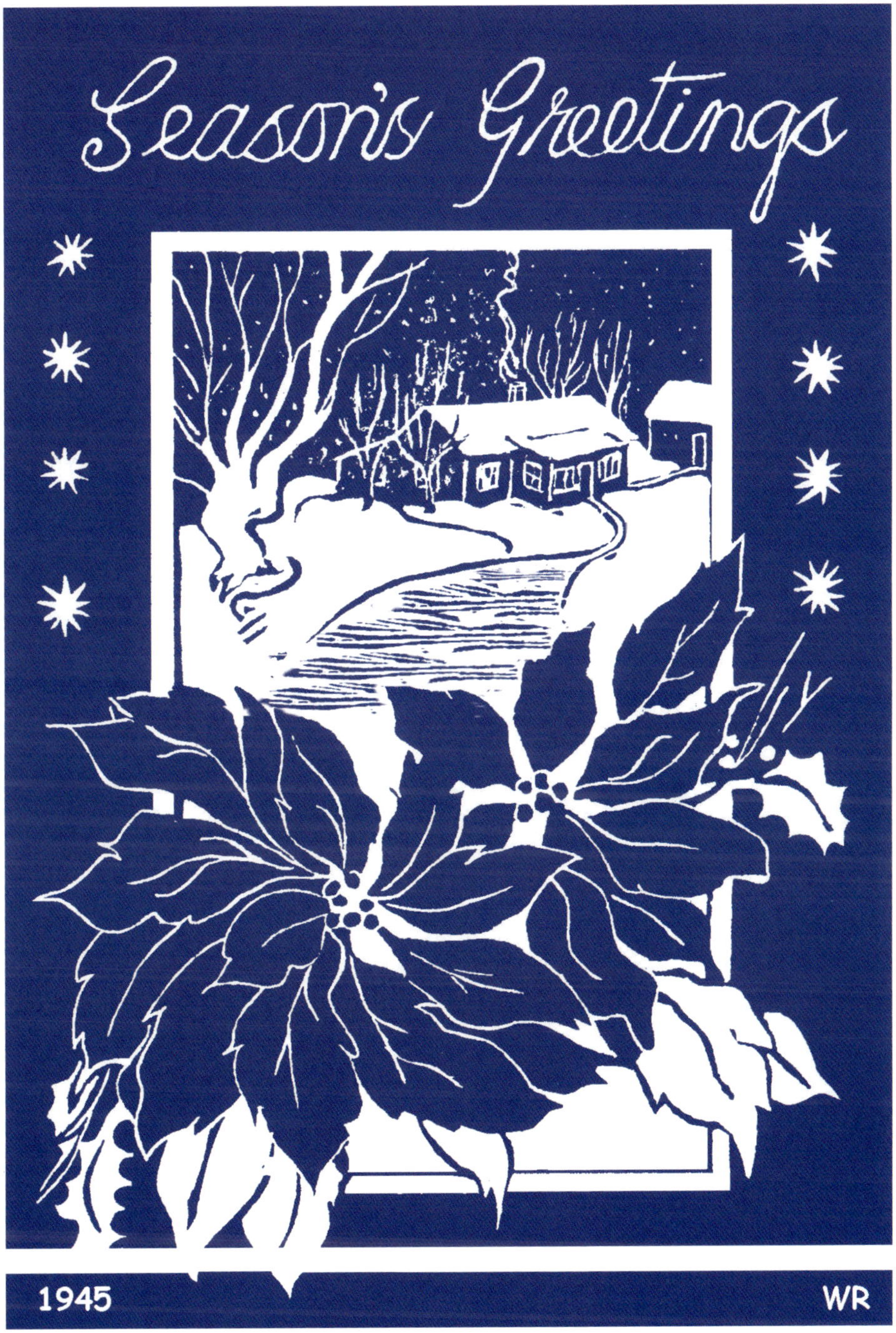
Season's Greetings
1945
WR

SNOWBOUND
1946

Off to the "big city" of Saskatoon for the rest of my high school, I had the remarkably good fortune of being enrolled in a special art class under the famous Austrian artist-teacher, Ernest Lindner. Even though the late Mr. Lindner exhibited in New York and other world centres, his innate humility and his empathy for young students were constants of his generous personality. One of his chief interests outside of painting and large-scale murals was graphics, including woodcuts, stone lithography and linocuts.

This two-block linocut perhaps reveals a few of the results of good teaching! The wind-sculpted snowdrifts and the hoarfrosted trees show at least some sensitivity to the Saskatchewan winter environment.

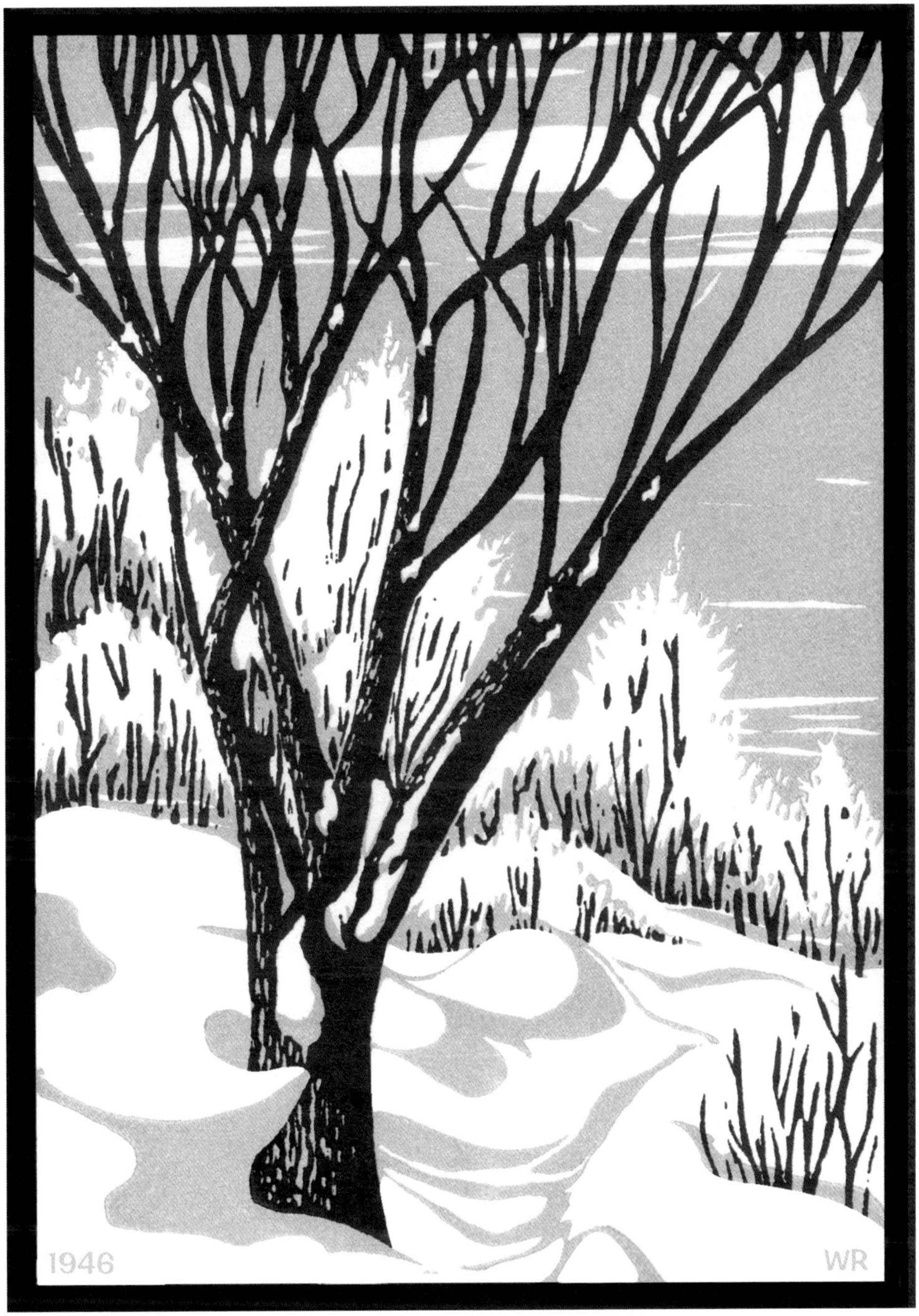
1946
WR

PRAIRIE SNOWDRIFTS
1947

At the advanced age of eighteen and in grade 12, I produced this single block linocut—once again revealing my fascination with the wind-sculpted snowdrifts of Saskatchewan. At this point I made quite frequent train trips back and forth to the old farm where my parents still lived. In this little linocut I also tried in a somewhat unsophisticated way to show the ever changing landscape—as viewed through the train window.

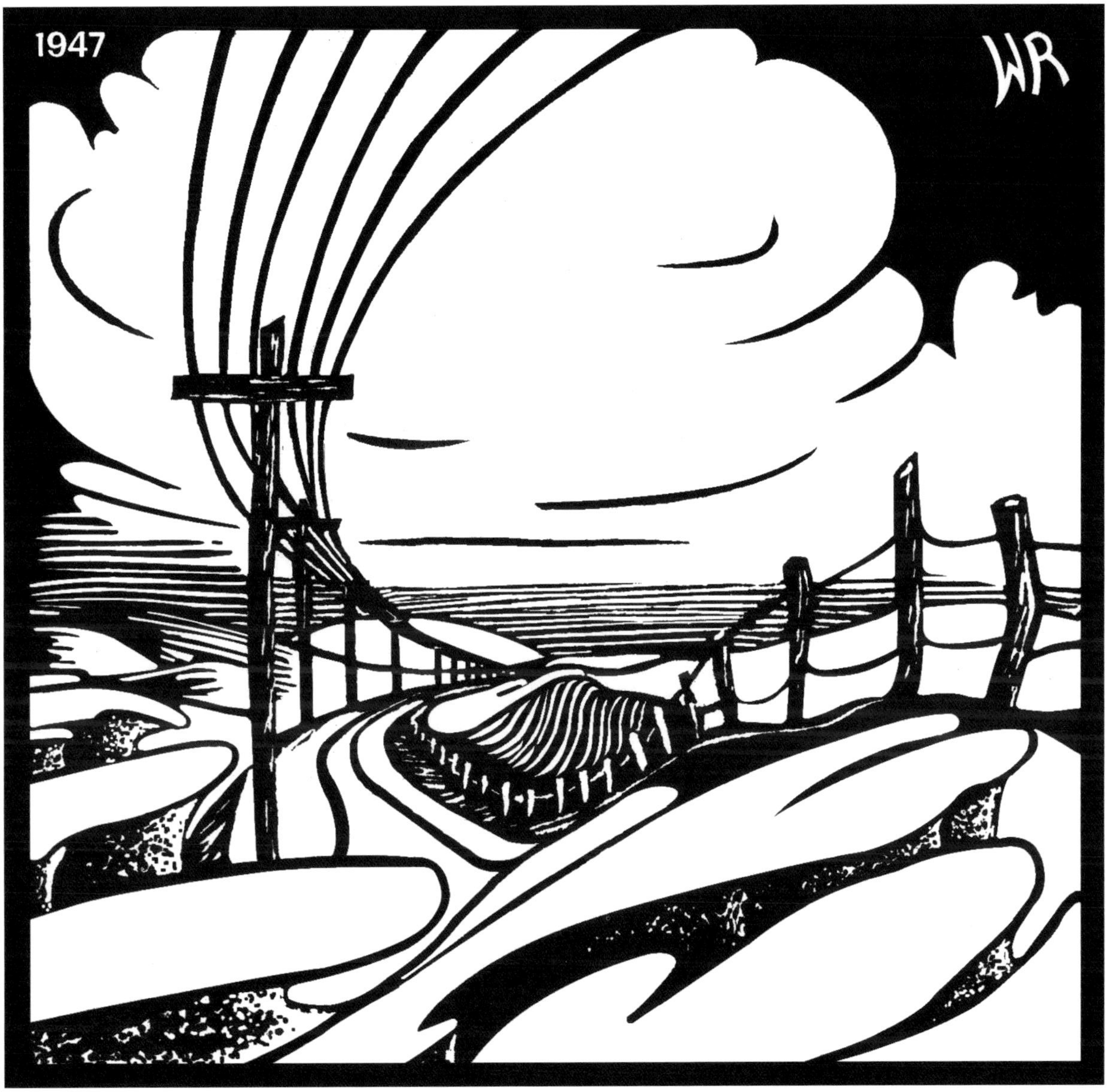
1947
WR

THE MOUNTAINS OF VANCOUVER
1949

A year in Vancouver with Aunt Lill was a stimulating time for me at age twenty. Still under a half million people and with few traffic problems, Vancouver was as attractive as Saskatoon with the added feature of a mountain backdrop, which seemed so close—even in Kitsilano where we lived. Although the weather was mild, I never quite got used to the constant fog and rain during the winter I was there.

In this two-block linocut I tried to show the beauty of cloud and fog swirling down, shrouding both the mountains and the houses below.

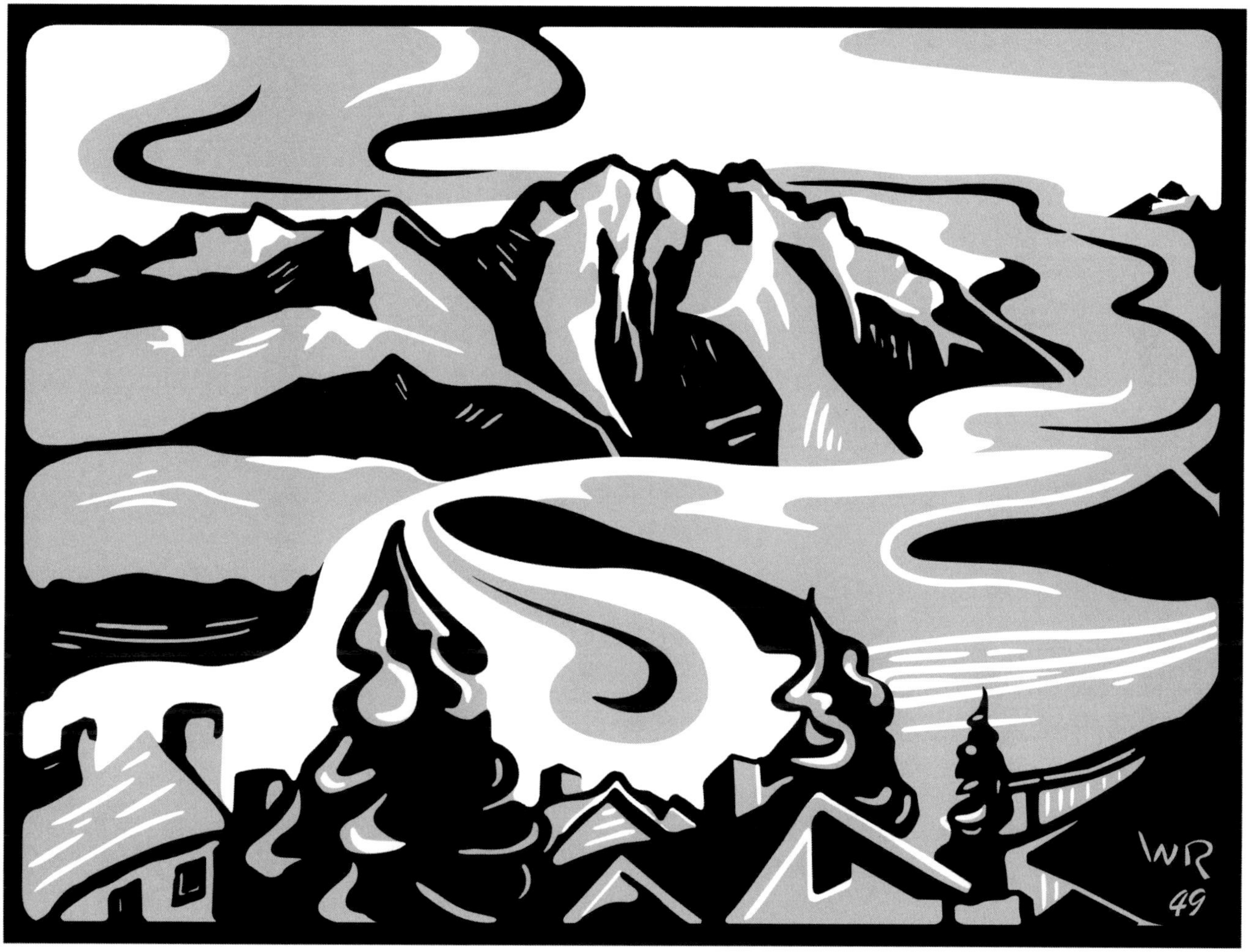
WR
49

MEADOW LAKE GRAIN ELEVATORS
1953

Grain elevators, the unique symbols of our once-thriving grain industry, are fast disappearing from the prairie landscape, to be replaced by a few widely spaced, large and undistinguished steel and concrete structures.

Teaching in Meadow Lake, Saskatchewan, I was impressed with this town's long row of huge wooden elevators with their many and varied "annexes". In retrospect, I realize that Meadow Lake had one of the largest grain storage capacities in Saskatchewan.

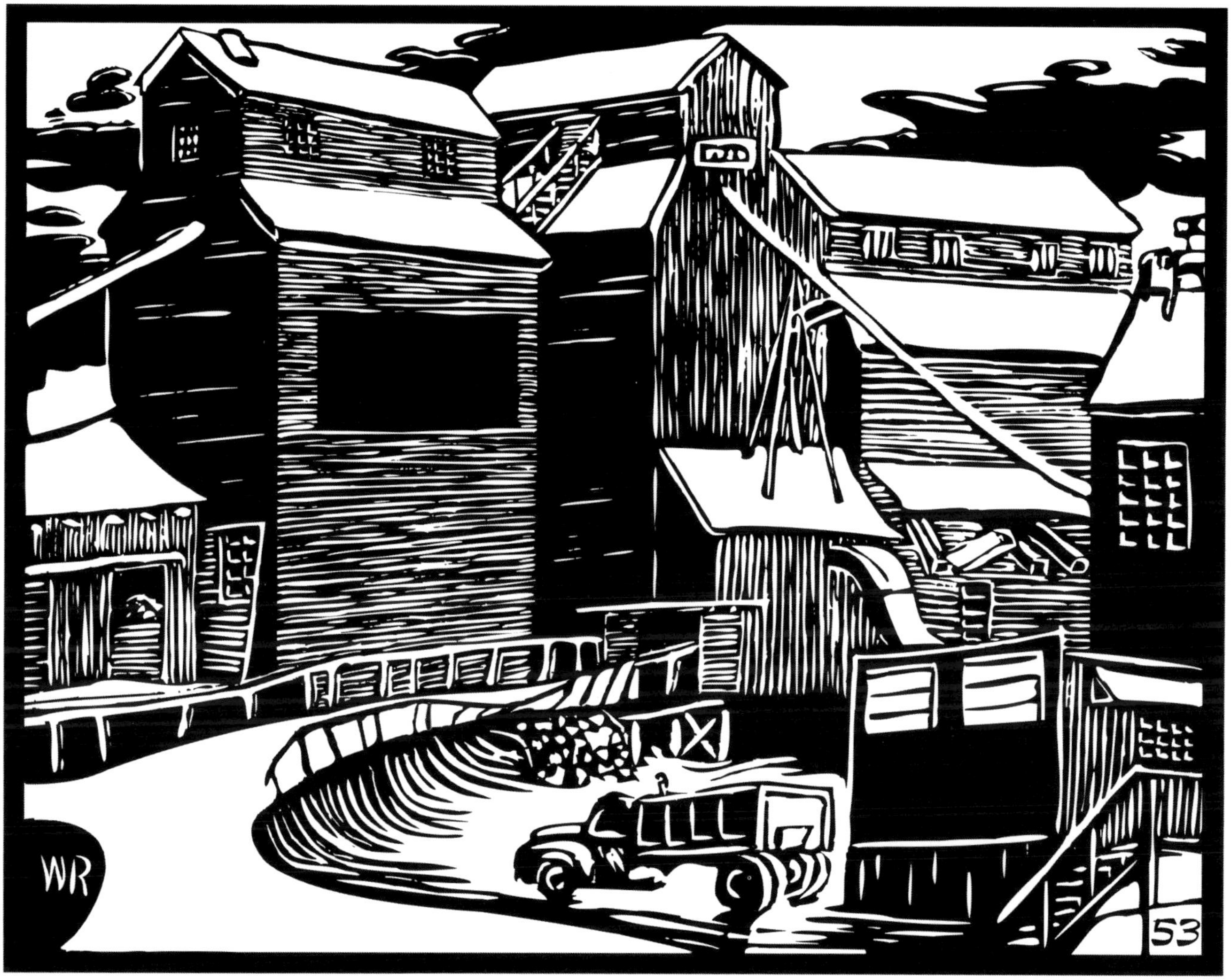
WR
53

AWAY IN A MANGER
1954

This one-block linocut depicting a conventional Christmas theme is perhaps one of my most successful attempts at simplicity and respect for the constraints and strengths of block printing.

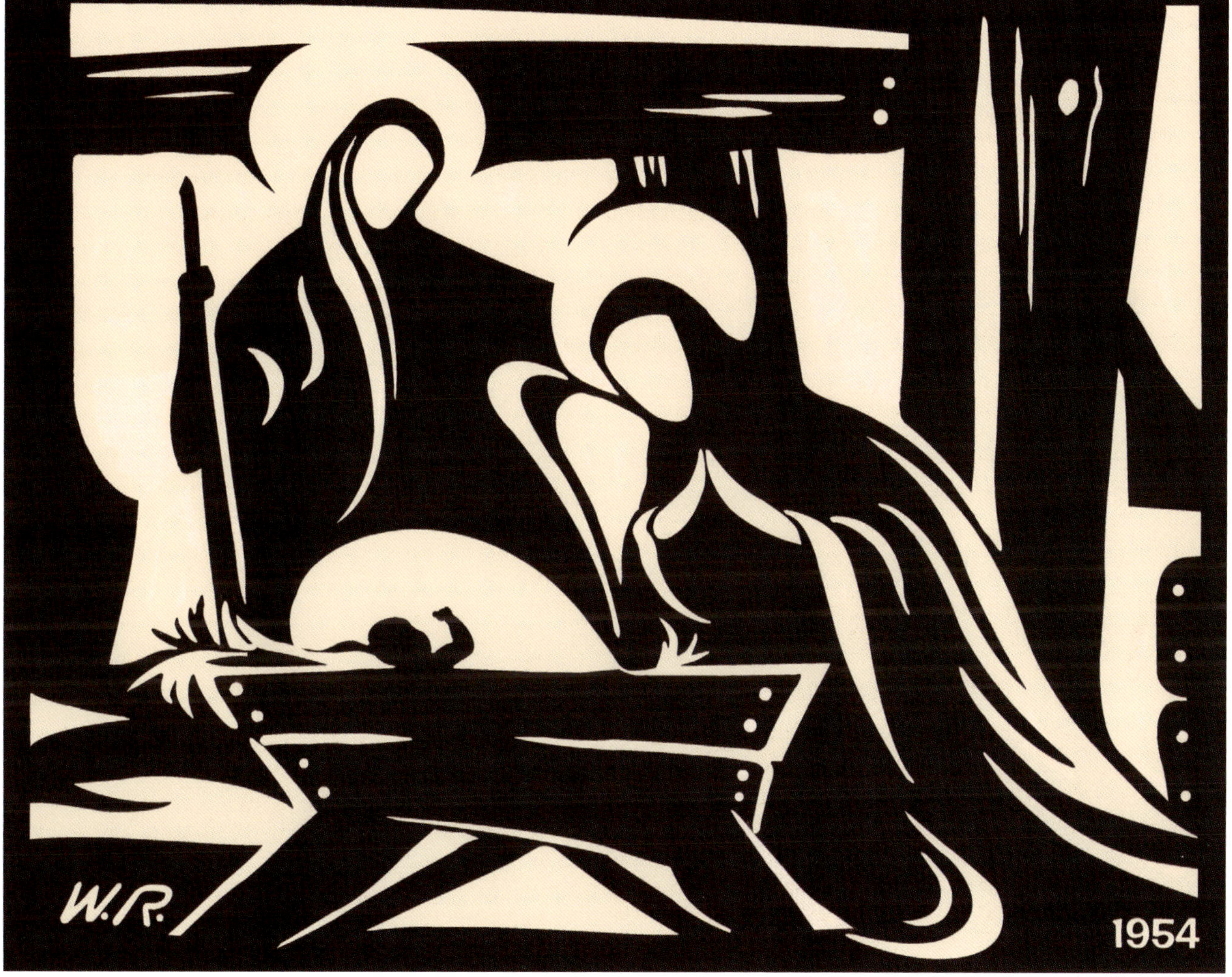
W.R.
1954

CHRIST IN CHRISTMAS
1955

This single-block linocut, somewhat more complicated than the previous manger scene, still retains the basic strength of a simple medium. My youthful idealism back in 1955 is quite obvious in the theme of this card, and is probably still applicable nowadays: Amid all the tinsel and hype of the Christmas season, we often forget that what we are really celebrating is the birth of a little baby—Jesus Christ.

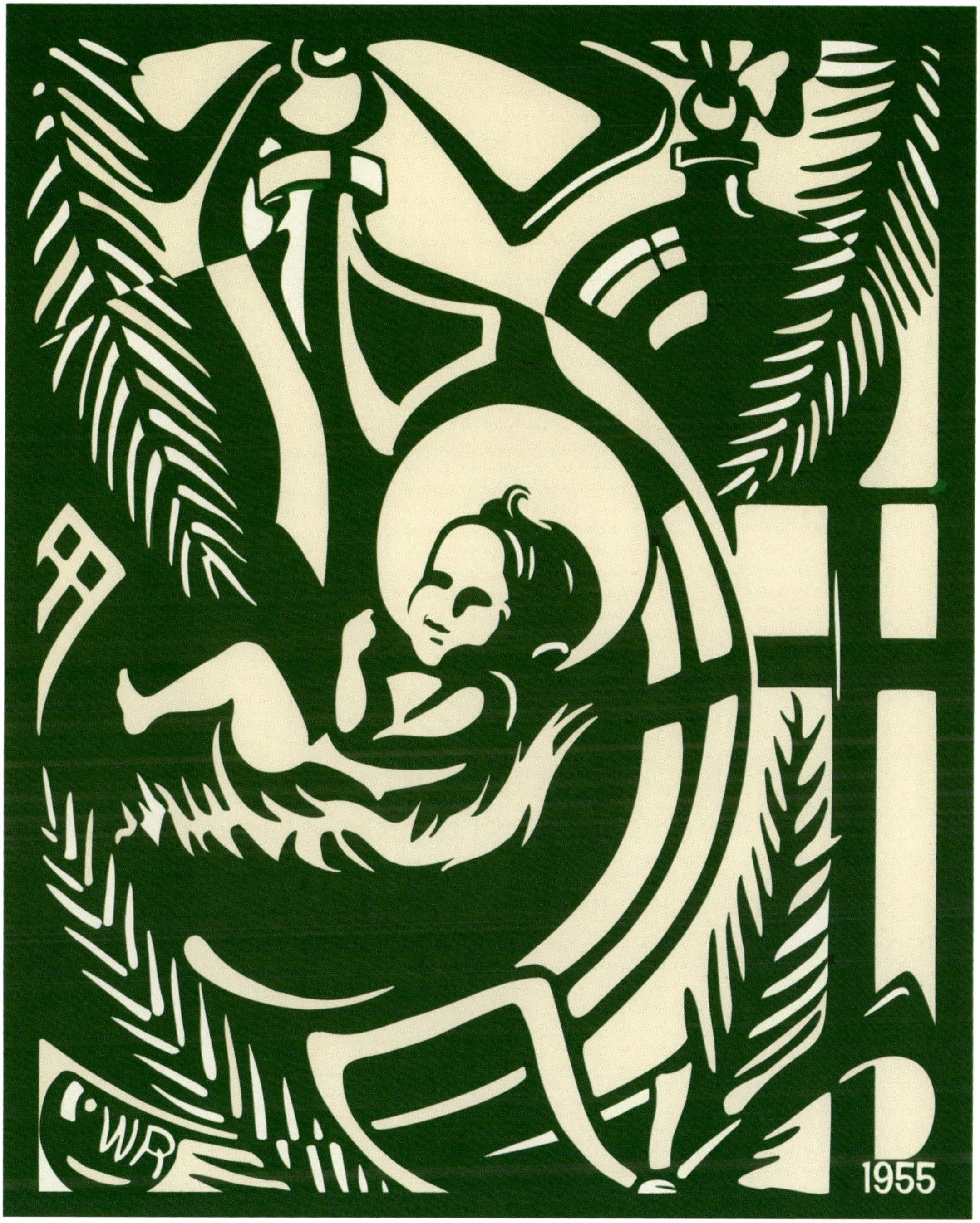
WR
1955

NORTHERN LIGHTS
1956

One of the many attractions in the northern forest country of Saskatchewan is the frequent and vivid appearance of the northern lights. This particular scene was inspired by a spectacular display my brother Frank and I witnessed as we were nearing Meadow Lake on a drive back from Saskatoon. We stopped the car at a midpoint in the 80 kilometre stretch of heavy forest south of town. Here, isolated from all human habitation, the "aurora borealis" seemed to dominate the whole scene.

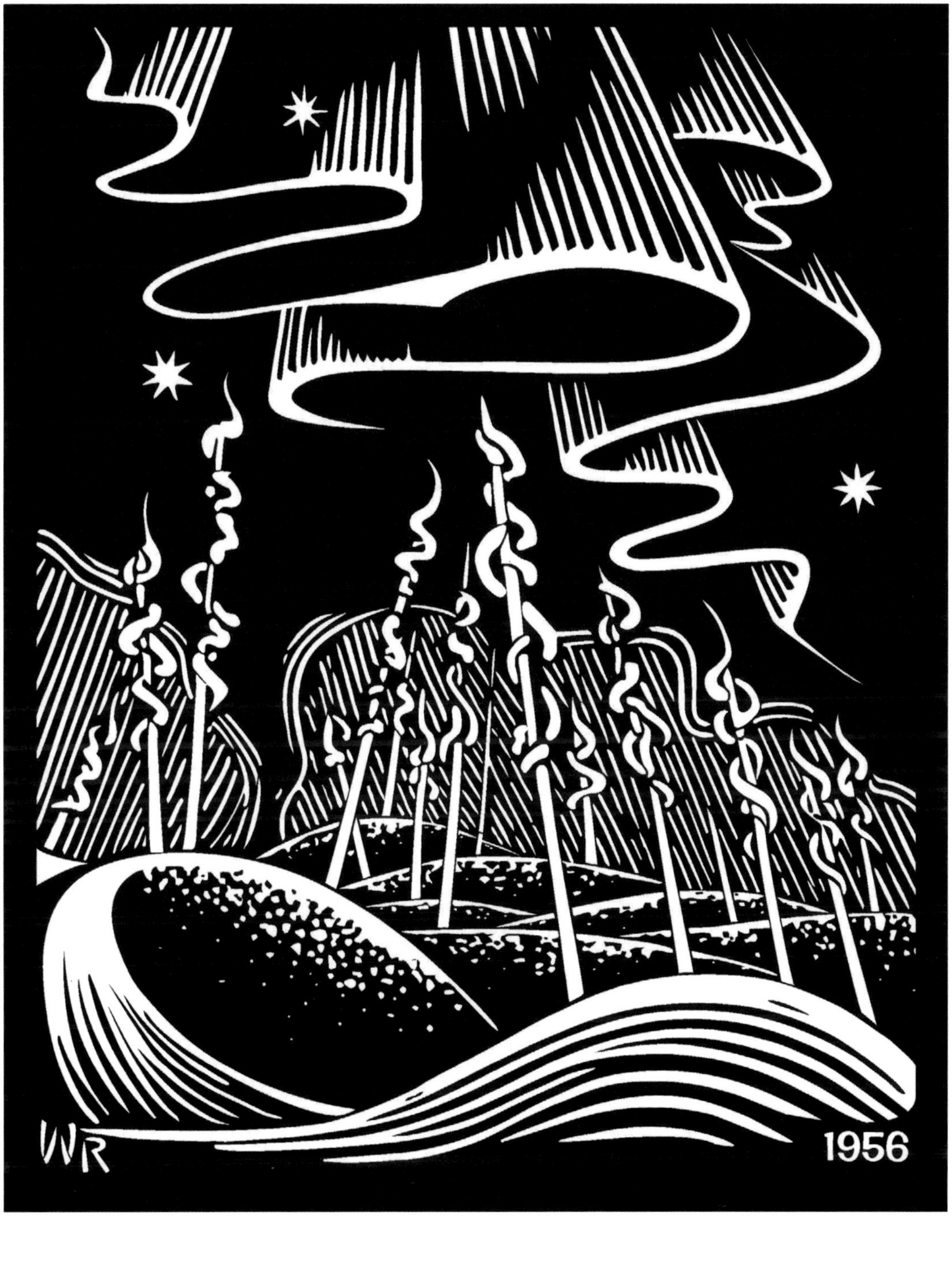
WR
1956

WOODSMAN
1957

Who among us has not at times envisioned being a woodsman living with his family in a simple log cabin in peace, quiet and contentment, "Far From the Madding Crowd"? Perhaps this is the kind of Christmas I longed for in 1957.

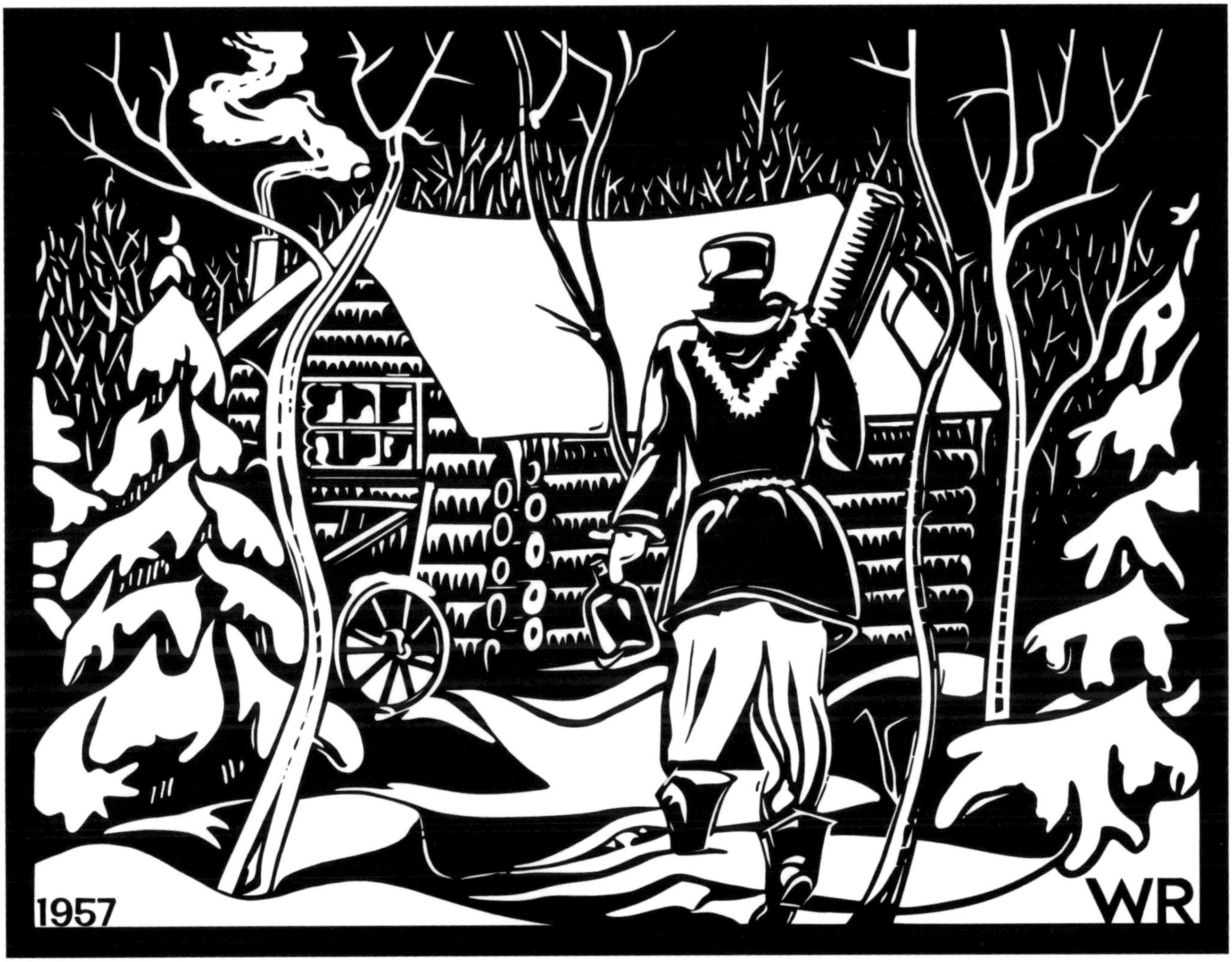
1957
WR

RCAF STATION COLD LAKE
1961

My marriage to Heidi and our move to RCAF Station Cold Lake marked the beginning of a fulfilling life with the Canadian air force.

At eighteen I painted the tempera picture, *Prairie Sentinels* (reproduced on p 88) depicting not only the two lone grain elevators at Tullis, Saskatchewan, but also a "condensation" of all the surrounding geographical features such as the Coteau Hills, twenty kilometres away, and even the planets circling overhead in the vaulted sky.

Here, fourteen years later, in this linocut, I have attempted another "geographical condensation" to encompass the entirety of the largest Canadian air base in one design—the PMQs (houses), the hangars, the CF100s flying overhead, the searchlights and even the trees and roadways.

RCAF Station Cold Lake is also the first (and last) three-block linocut I designed. Here there was one block for the dark blue, one for the light blue and a third for the yellow. The problem, as with any multicolor graphic, is the accurate registration of the "overprints".

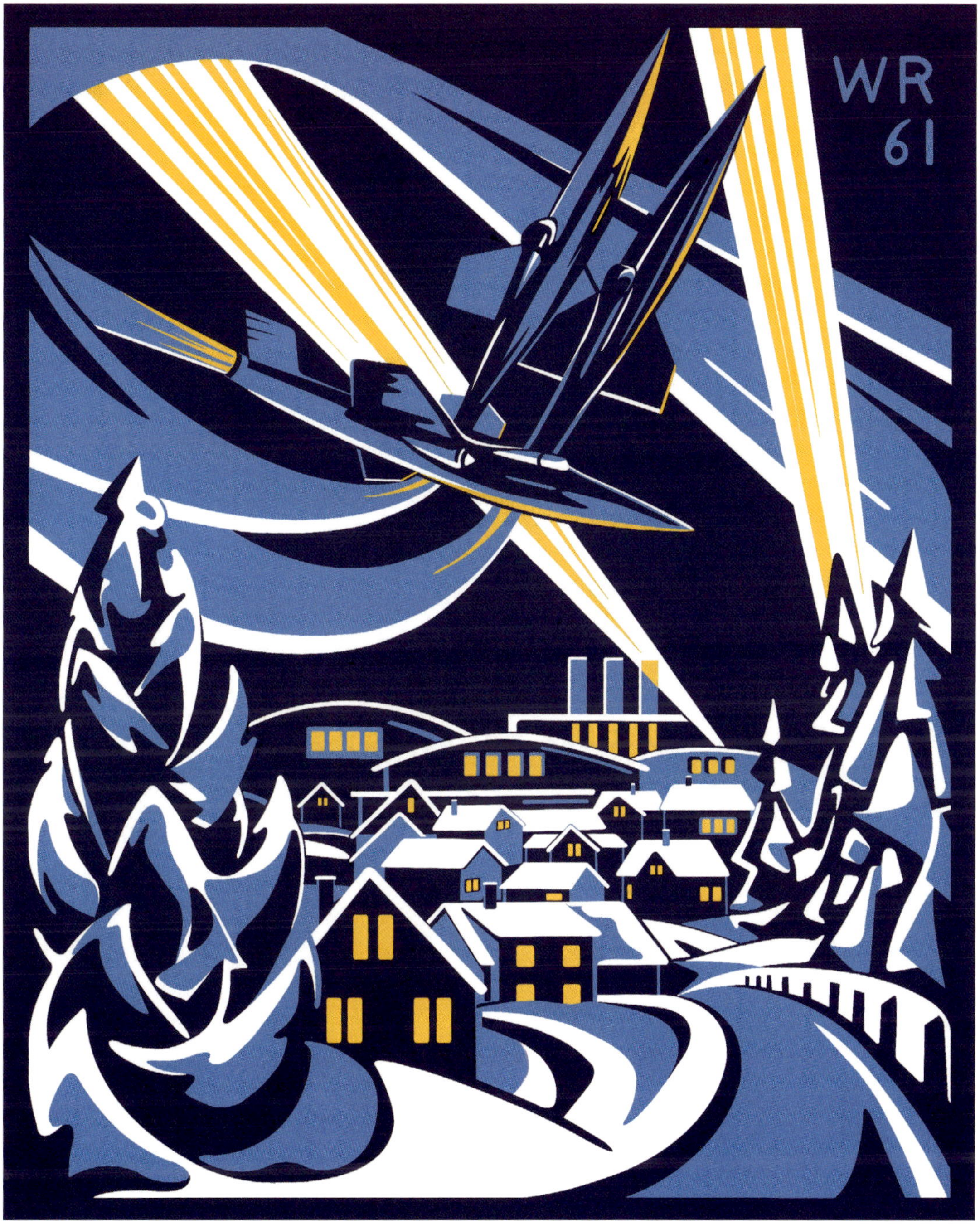
WR
61

AFRICAN MADONNA
1962

Martin Luther King delivered his famous "I have a dream" speech in Washington in 1963. During the late 50s and throughout the 60s the struggle for racial equality loomed large in United States and was at the forefront of political concerns in both the United States and Canada.

In 1962 I chose motherhood, the most fundamental human state of all races and creeds, as the theme for this linocut.

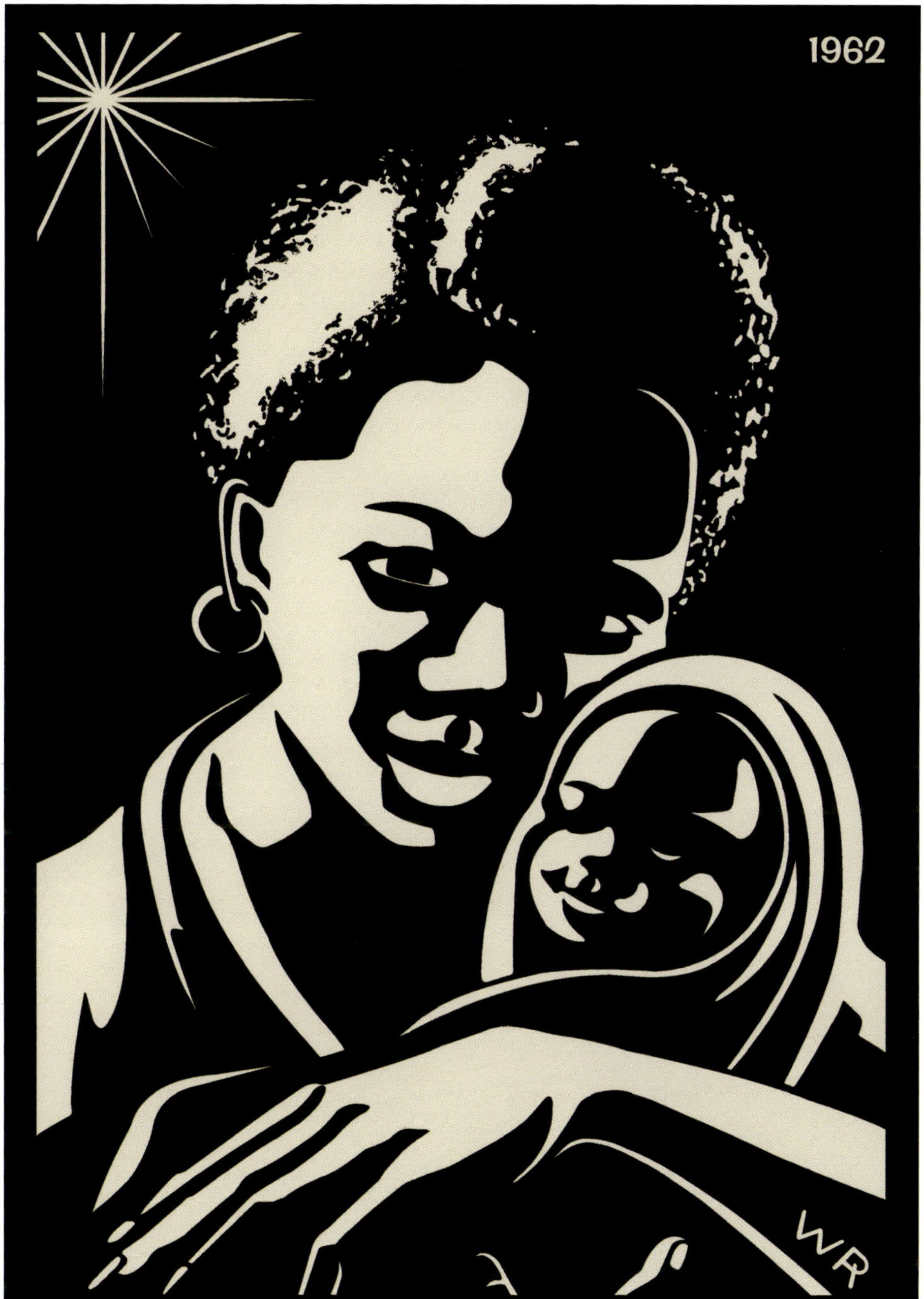
1962
WR

The 25 Christmas cards featured on pp 38 – 87 are all serigraphs. The serigraph or “silk screen print” is produ using the basic principle of an ordinary stencil. The process involves forcing thick inks through a fine silk or present-day synthetic fabric which has been stretched tightly on a strong wooden frame. The first step is to ma a stencil or to produce it photographically. (The photographic method is essentially a commercial approach.) I important to remember that the stencil is designed to stop ink passing through the screen except in the open ar of the design which have been cut out. Mostly, I used the hand-cut lacquer stencil, and sometimes in addition, “touché technique” which involves applying a blocking liquid with a paint brush directly to the screen. After stencil is cut, it is adhered to the screen by partially dissolving it into the fabric. The hinged screen is lowered o the cut stencil. The solvent is then applied to the screen using a ball of soft cloth which is kept moistened to “right” degree with the solvent. Moderate pressure must be applied to force the solvent through the screen to stencil below. Attaching the stencil is a very tricky part of the process, especially with intricate stencils, as it is too easy to wash out important detail.

BASIC SILK SCREEN (SERIGRAPH) EQUIPMENT

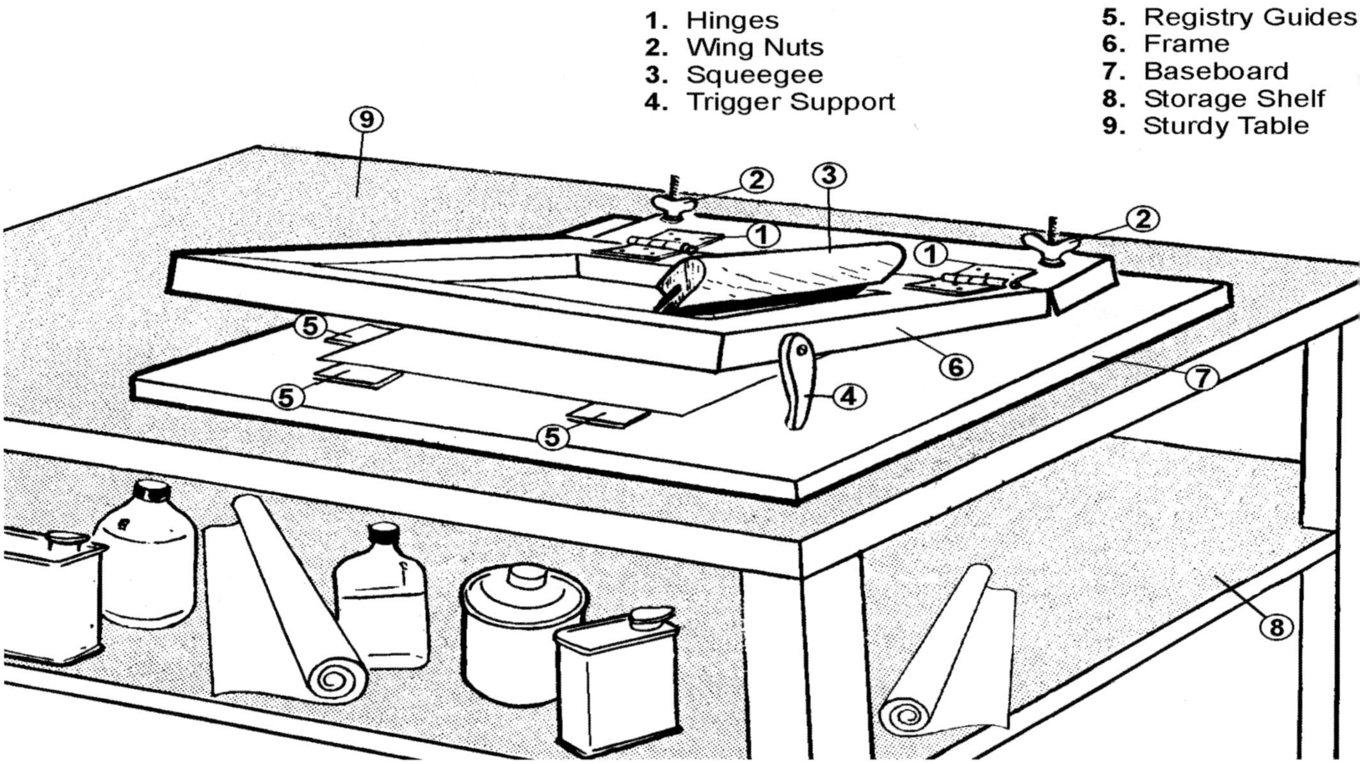

hen the stencil has adhered and has been properly sealed at the edges, the frame is lowered on its hinges over
: heavy paper or other material to be printed. A long bead of ink poured out at one end of the screen is then
·ced through the spaces not masked by the stencil—using a specially designed **squeegee** which is like a "heavy
ty" windshield wiper. The ink, of course penetrates the fabric only where the stencil has been cut out or left
ınk. When the frame is lifted, the design has been printed on the paper; the process may be repeated until a
mber of prints has been produced. For **multicolored prints** such as these Christmas cards, as many as six or

4-SCREEN OVERPRINTING

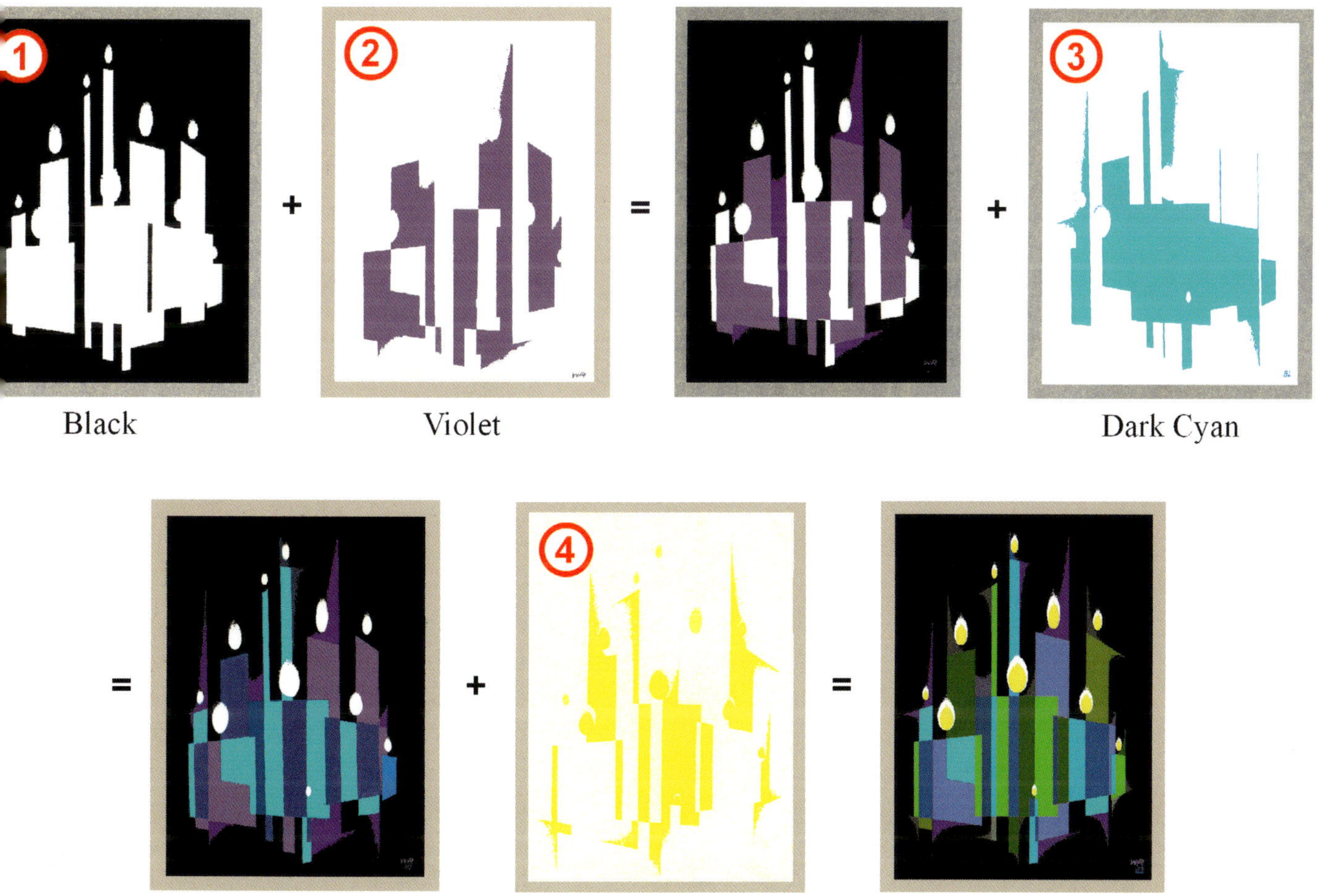

(See pp72-73)

more printings or **over-printings** are required for each card, using an entirely new stencil for each successive pri ing, as can be seen in the 4-screen chart shown on the previous page. Precision and careful planning are critic The most difficult matter is **registration**—printing on exactly the right part of the previously printed (and dri design. Usually, tolerances cannot exceed one-half millimetre. Achieving precisely the correct degree of ink **tra parency** is another critical matter in overprinting. For example, an opaque vermilion printed over black wo produce a "burnt orange" color; whereas, a more transparent vermilion would produce a rich terra cotta brov Multicolored printing has to be planned and orchestrated with patience and continuous attention to many detail

Serigraph prints are noted for strong outlines and clear, brilliant hues not possible with other printing metho However, somewhat softer effects are possible, if desired in parts of a design, using the touché method as I with the hoarfrosted trees in *Heavy Oil* on p 85. Another device to produce shading or softness I "pioneered" a developed, myself. This technique consisted of using punches ground from hypodermic needles to produce sm closely spaced holes in the stencil. Varying the size of the hypodermic punch holes and the spacing between th produced the "shading". This experimental shading method was used in *Candelabrum* on p 73, with big punches in *Carol of the Bells* on p 77, and in *Northern Lights* on p 82. Another example is the larger serigra *Hoarfrost*, reproduced on p viii, but not used as a Christmas card.

One of the most challenging techniques to master in serigraph production is the "squeegee blend" used to produ soft gradations from one color to another. The technique was used horizontally and vertically in *Forty Below* p 41, and at two different angles and with three or four different colors in *Northern Lights* on p 83. The colo inks to be blended are poured directly onto the sealed border area of the screen, then mixed and blended wit painting knife. Next, several trial prints on scrap paper are produced with the squeegee until the desired blenc achieved. At this point regular printing can proceed until the ink runs out or the colors have become too blurr The screen is then cleaned and the process to establish the blend is repeated.

Perhaps it was my Scottish ancestral blood, or perhaps just my methodical nature, but in serigraphy I was m intrigued with the process of over-printing because with only a few screens a number of extra colors could produced at a saving in time and the cost of ink! Because I usually worked with a liquid emulsifier and real color pigments to produce my inks, I was able to experiment with regulating transparency. Gradually, with mu trial and error, I learned enough about transparence to use overprinting quite effectively. A side benefit of t over-printing was that applying inks over one another usually produced a very satisfactory harmony in the ove color scheme of the print. On the next page is a plan for overprinting in the serigraph, *Grain Elevators*. In t sequence 5 screens have produced (counting the paper) 16 quite subtle colors!

Modern serigraph printing developed from the ancient Chinese and Japanese art of stencil painting. With pho graphic stencil production, the serigraph is probably the most common type of printing in industry for such thi as the intricate dials in an aircraft or the less exact designs on textiles or cardboard boxes. In the last half cent the serigraph has become an important fine art as well. Nearly every modern gallery displays serigraph pri along with the older graphics such as woodcuts, lithographs, or etchings.

PALETTE and PRINTING SEQUENCE for *GRAIN ELEVATORS, p 70-71*

ORDER of PRINTING	SCREEN COMBO	VALUE SCALE	COLOR DESCRIPTION	PIGMENTS
1	1	1	Black	Ivory Black (opaque)
	1+2	2	Dark Indian Red	
	1+3	3	Dark Terra Cotta	
	1+2+3	4	Terra Cotta	
	1+4	5	Dark Ochre	
	1+3+4	6	Medium Brown	
	1+4+5	7	Medium Ochre	
	1+3+4+5	8	Ochre	
2	2	9	Cool Red	Napthol Crimson + Cadmium/Barium Red. Med.
	2+3	10	Red-red-orange	
3	3	11	Red-orange	Cadmium/Barium Red, Lt.
	3+4	12	Orange-red-orange	
4	4	13	Orange	Hansa Orange
	4+5	14	Yellow-orange	
5	5	15	Warm Yellow	Cadmium Yellow, Deep
	0	16	White (paper)	

FAMILY CHRISTMAS
1964

This first serigraph Christmas card captures a joyful part of one of those fleeting years when our children were little and the focus of our existence—the "best years of our lives"! Family life became even more fulfilling when a fourth child, our daughter, joined the clan in 1965.

With three screens, for black, lime, and flesh color, overprinting produced two additional colors: tan and forest green. The design was kept simple with a main emphasis on the lively antics of three boys aged 2, 3 and 4.

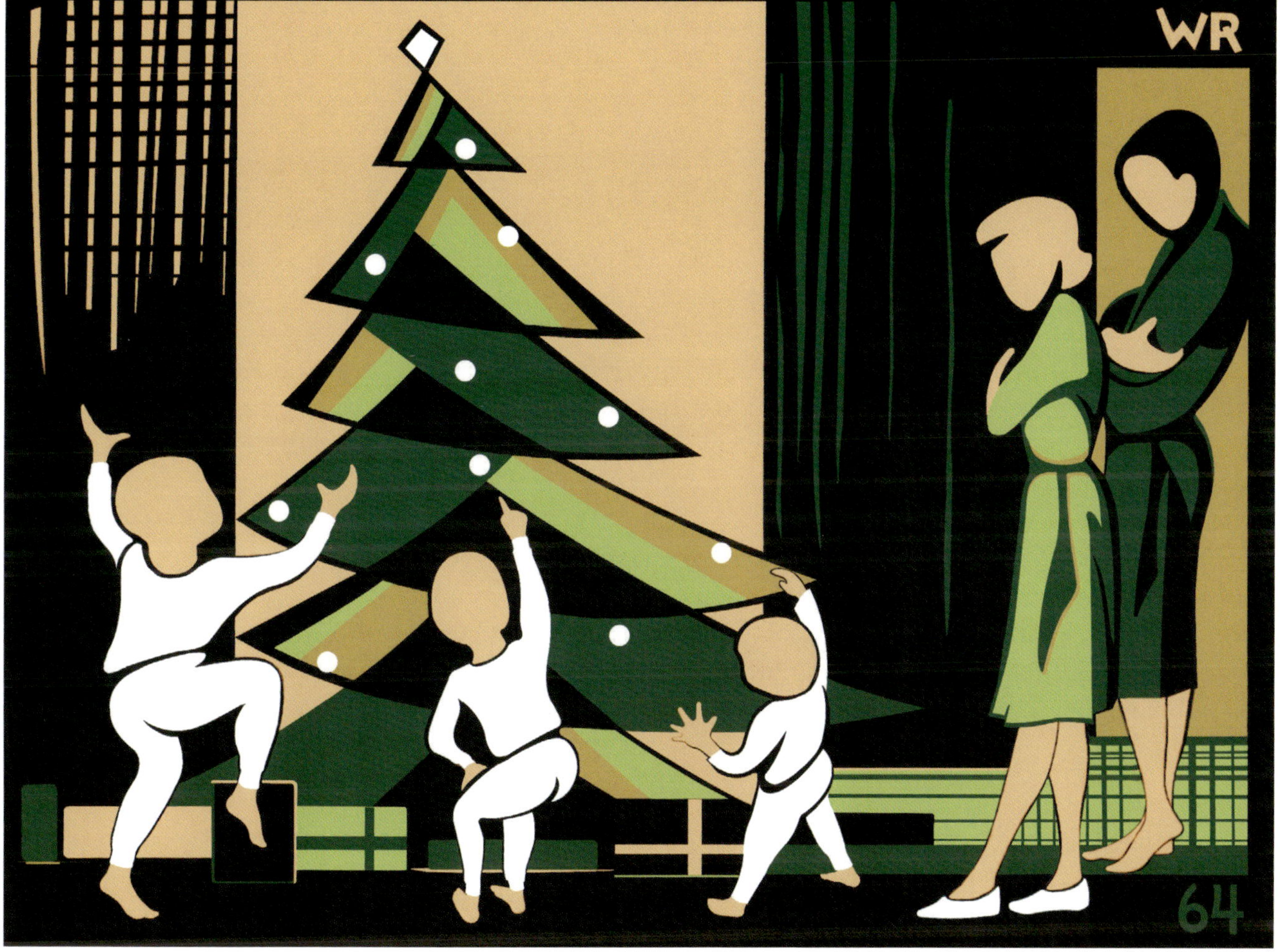
WR
64

FORTY BELOW
1965

Western Canadians who live a distance east of the Rockies and north of the fifty-fourth parallel know what it is like to survive those several forty-below days that usually descend on them each January. Living and adapting become an adventure which only well heated homes and heavy clothing can sustain.

This print recalls a typical calm, dark and frigid night at Canadian Forces Base Cold Lake, Alberta, when the steam from hundreds of toiling gas furnaces rises high and straight into the blue-black depths of the sky. The only warmth is in the brightly lit interiors of the houses.

Over the years I have twice repeated the theme of this 1965 Christmas card, first as an acrylic painting and second as the larger, more complicated serigraph shown here. This is one of my first attempts at using the rather difficult "squeegee blend" to produce the horizontal gradation in the sky and the vertical gradation in the window colors.

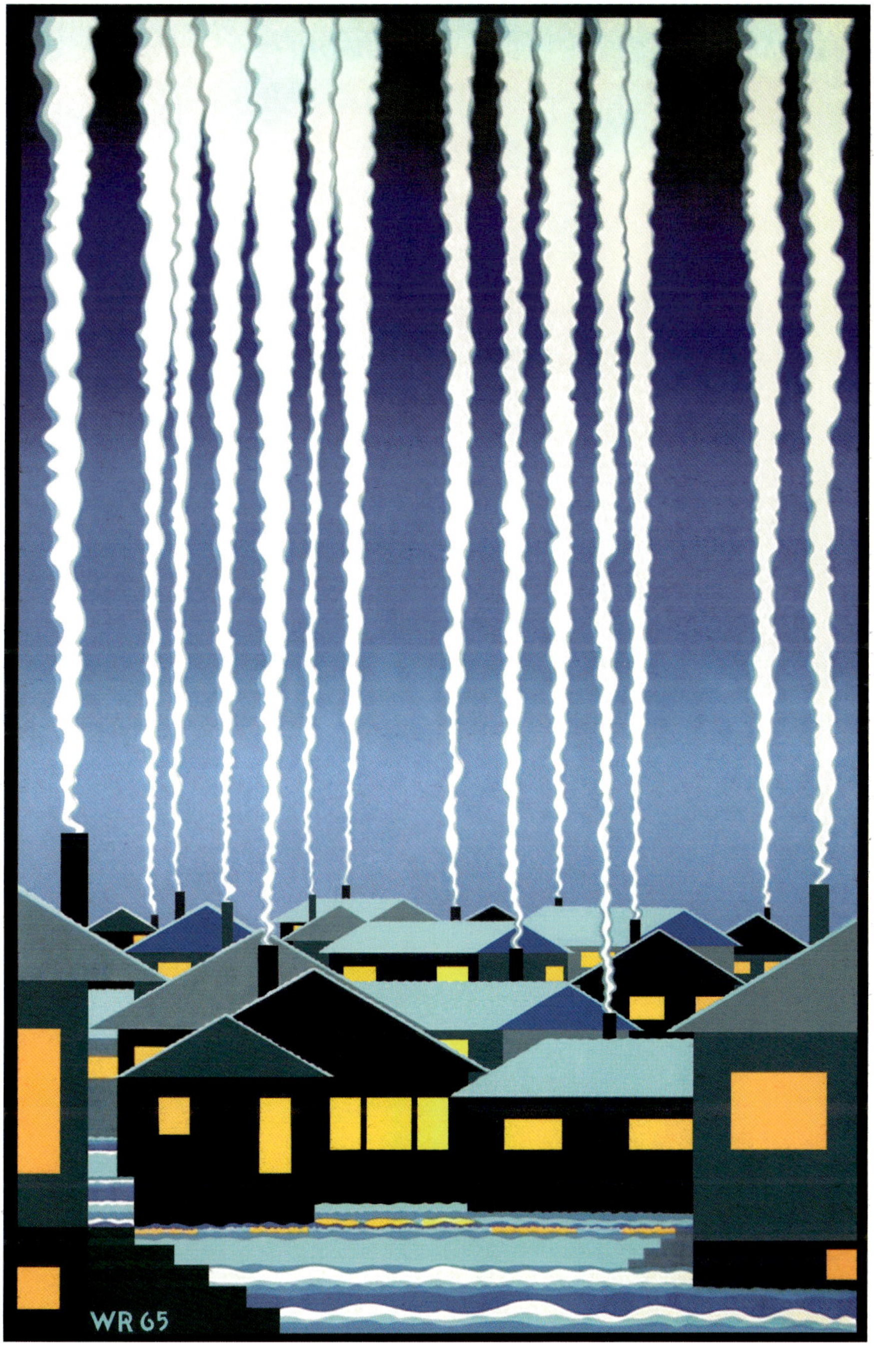
WR 65

AUTUMN FOREST
1966

As we continued to live in the boreal forest area of Alberta for many years, the splendor of the woods became one of my favorite themes for both painting and graphics. In this print I tried to show two aspects of trees—first, the diaphanous or translucent quality of fall trees, and second, the interrelationship and harmony in the various parts of trees: Trees are like leaves and leaves are like trees!

The several colors in this serigraph were achieved from the overprinting of the three screens, black, yellow and red.

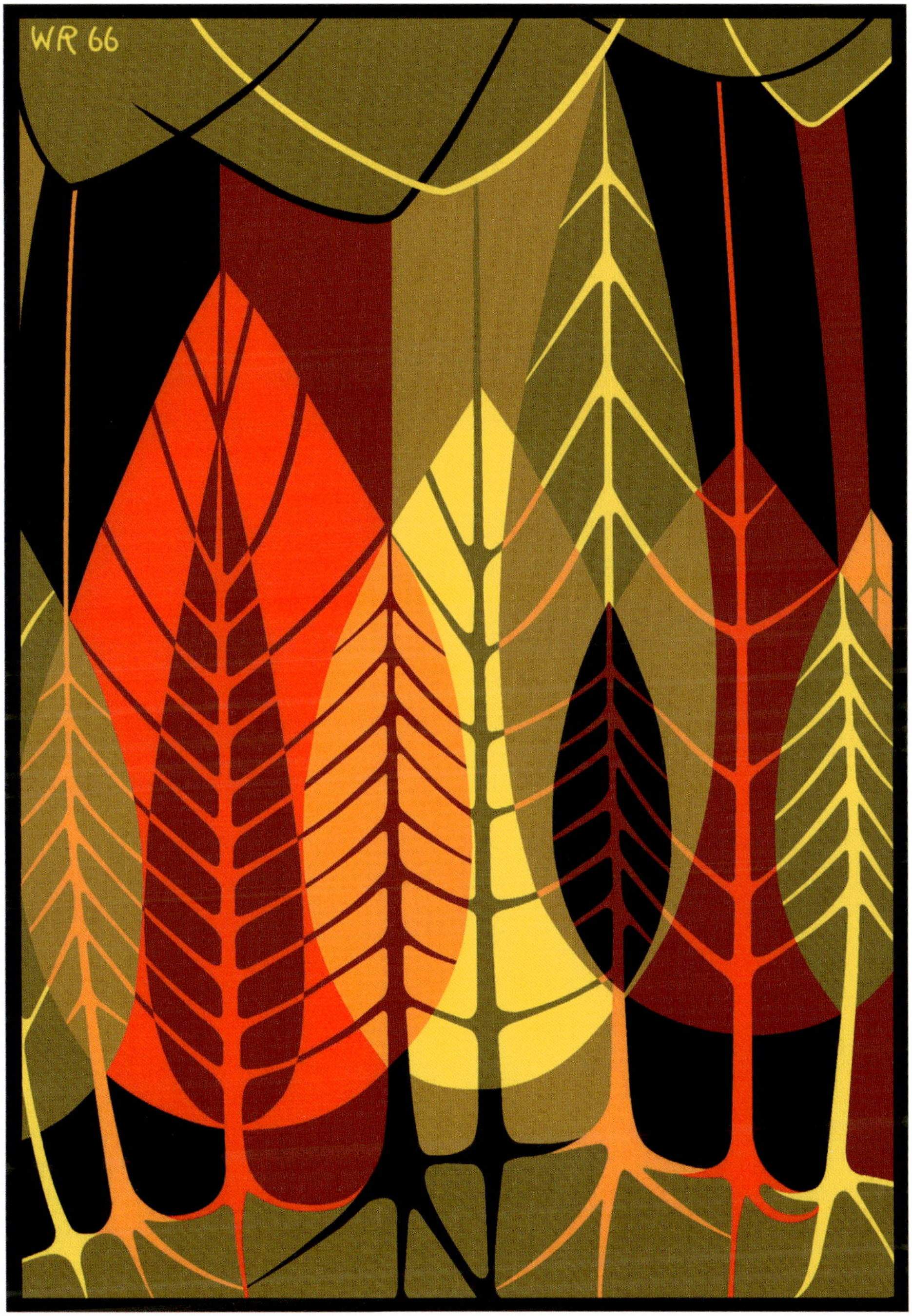
WR 66

GIVING
1967

"Noel" brings out one of the truly noble qualities in human nature—generosity, which, unfortunately, can be all too rare in our day-to-day lives the rest of the year. Sometimes at Christmas we even "give" outside our family circle, where the need is perhaps greater.

In this three-screen serigraph I have tried to convey, through hand gestures blended with the printed word, the gift of giving.

A few readers may remember the old grade one readers used in western Canadian schools during the 1930s and 40s. I chose the same three ink colors that were used to picture "Jerry and Jane" back then—black, orange and blue!

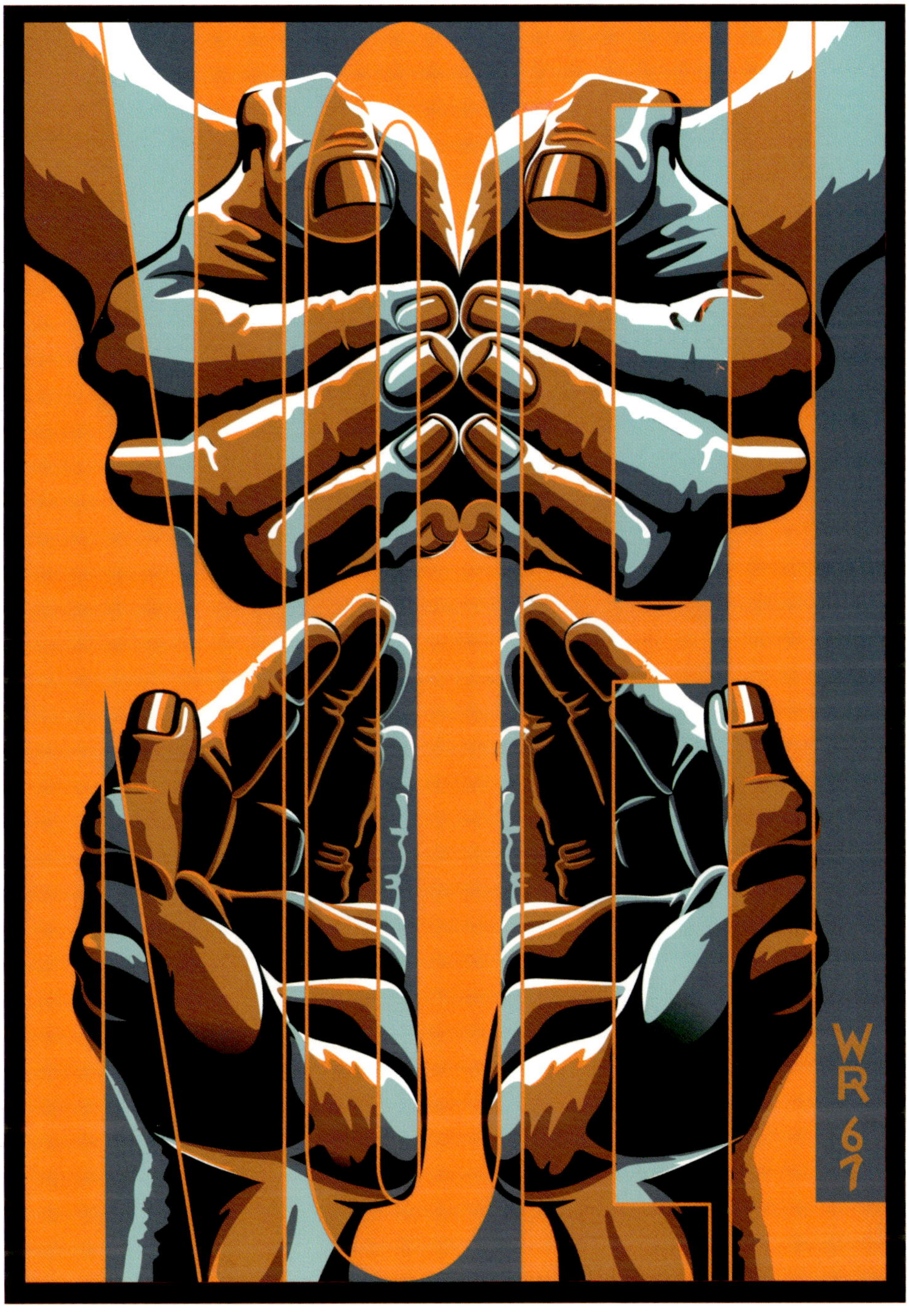
WR 67

THE ROCKIES
1968

Like most of us from the Prairies, I have driven through the Rockies many times, and continue to be impressed with the rugged character of these mountains. Here the beauty is strong and showy unlike the more subtle attractions of the vast, rolling prairies to the east.

In this print I have tried to capture the curvaceous rock structures of the Jasper area which, to me, are quite different from the more angular structures at Banff.

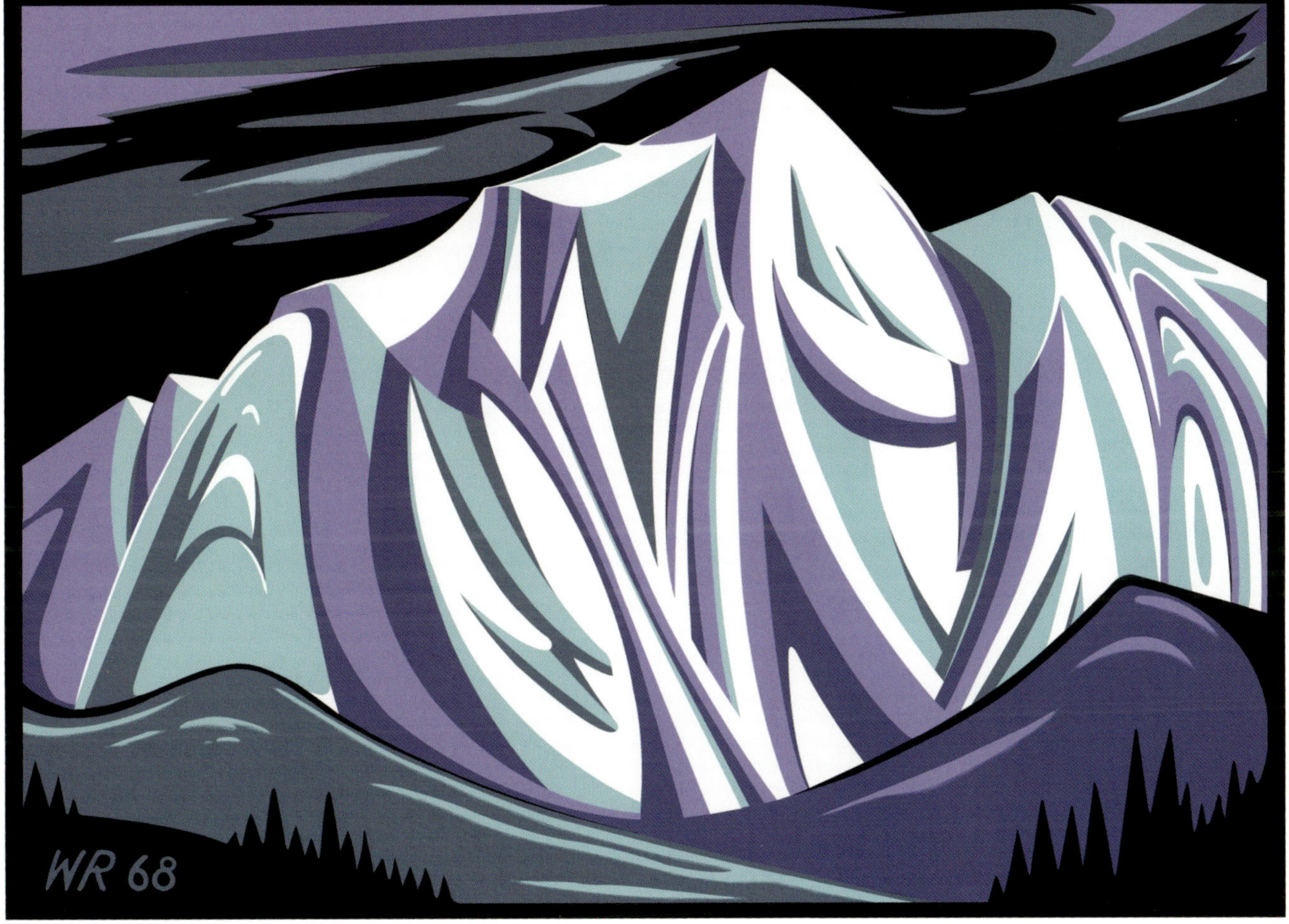
WR 68

KIDS DANCING
1969

In this serigraph, with simplified forms and colors, I have tried to capture the dizzying blur of excitement kids experience just before Christmas day. Here our daughter Margaret is giving her three brothers, Robin, Ryan and Patrick, a sample of her happy and continuing "me too" approach to family life.

The three transparent primary colors, red, yellow and blue, were used here in an "additive" way to produce two of the secondary colors, green and orange.

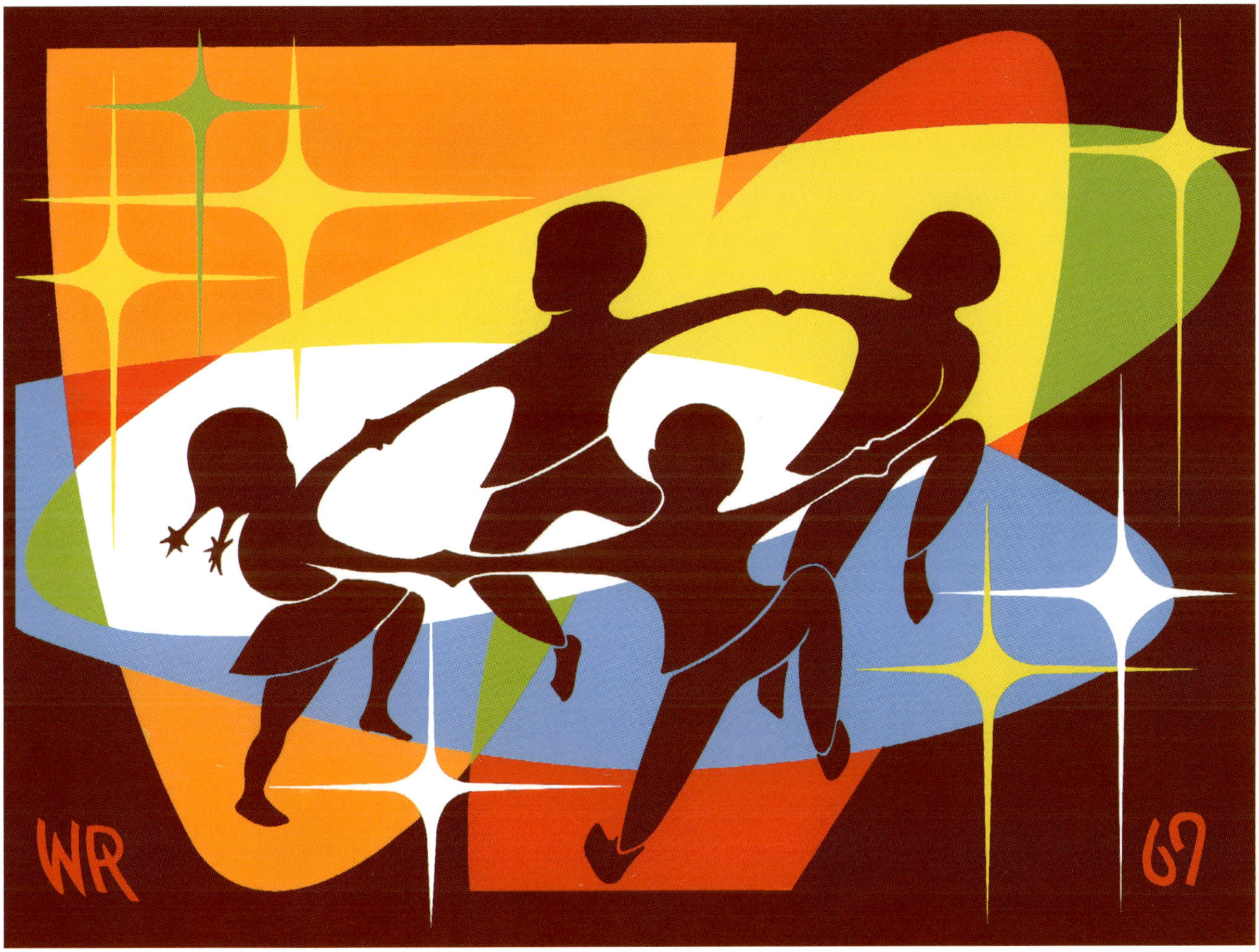
WR
69

A WALK IN THE WOODS
1970

For this print I combined two favorite subjects—family and forest. Perhaps there is a trace of Druidism in the portrayal of the woods at sunset as a great outdoor cathedral!

Both the design and the color scheme are a little more complicated this time. Four screens were used: vermilion, gold, a semi opaque powder blue, and black. Overprinting produced three additional colors: dark blue, tan, and rust.

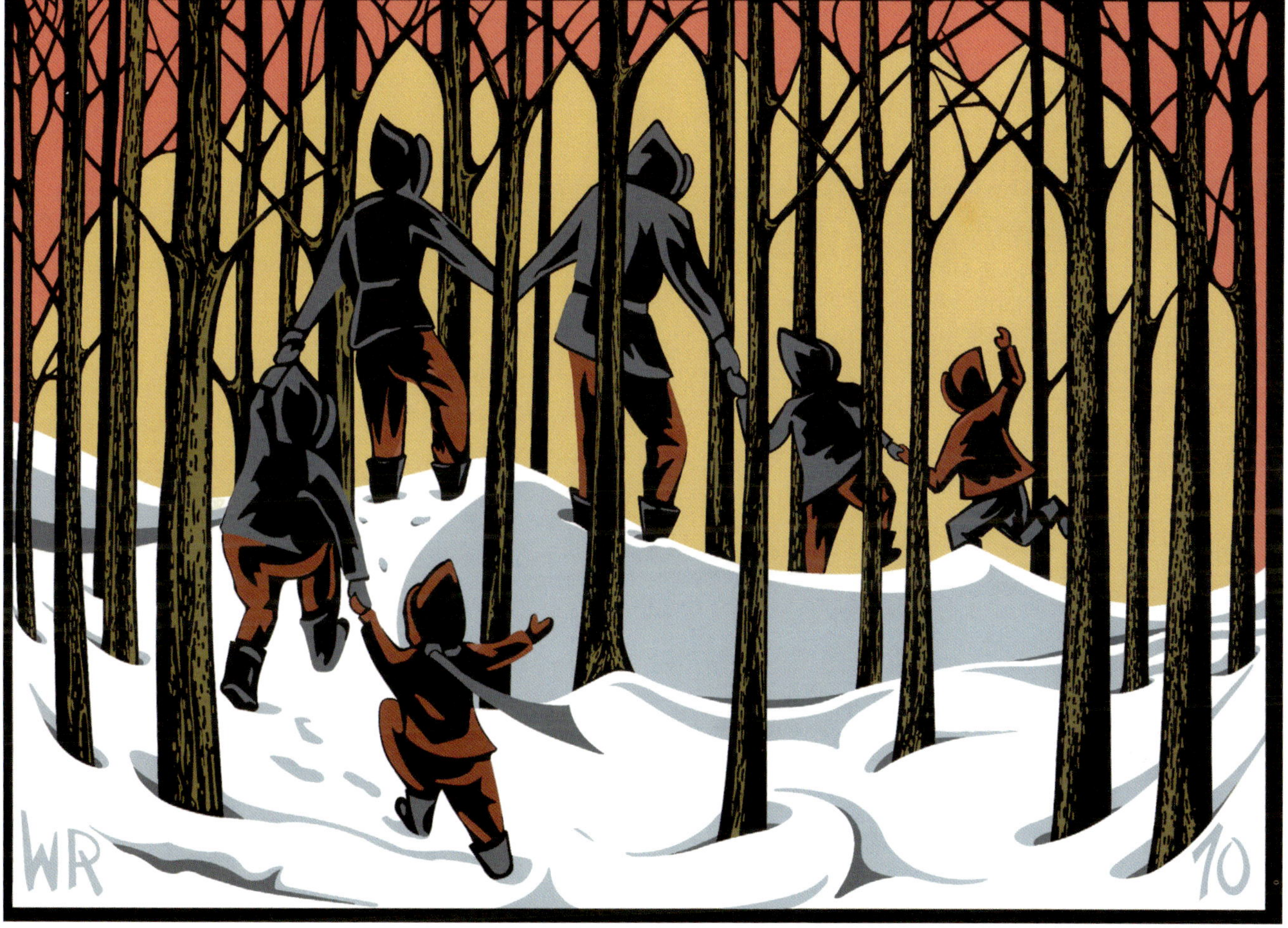
WR
10

BRASS BAND
1971

Always a lover of music, here I have attempted to portray in color the exciting sound of a brass band—to herald the arrival of Christmas.

The three screens used were cyan, magenta, and yellow, overlapping in an additive process similar to the industrial printing system known as CMYK (minus the "K" or black). In this way four bright secondary colors were added.

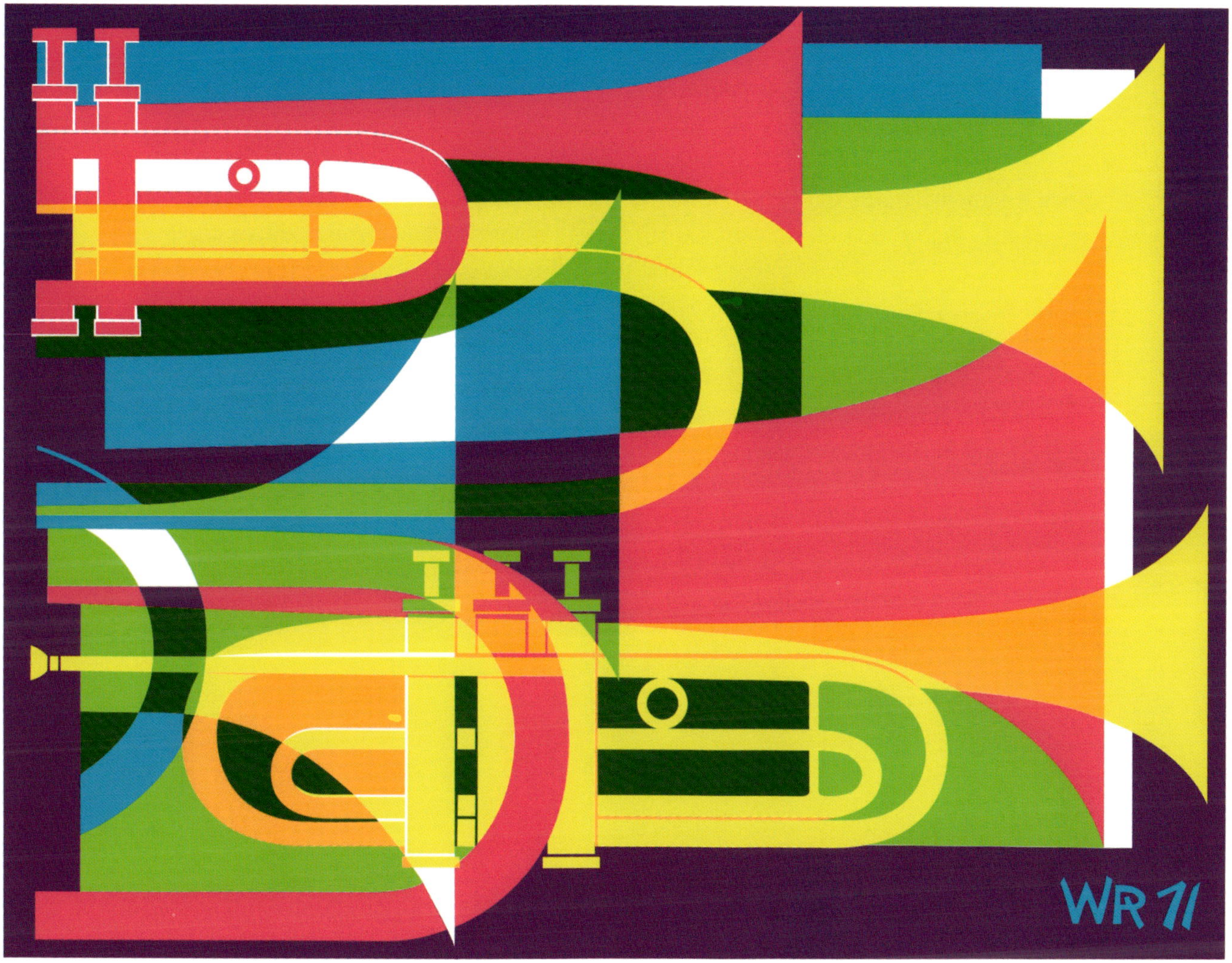
WR 71

FAMILY SILHOUETTE
1972

Once again my main interest—family—was the subject of our Christmas card. It was gratifying to me that this simple silhouette pleased so many of our friends, and that they were able to *recognize* each of the kids. We even received some praise for the aesthetics of the card; perhaps love and sincerity are prime ingredients in successful art!

Only two screens were used: black and a semi-opaque flesh color, which overprinted on the black to produce a warm grey.

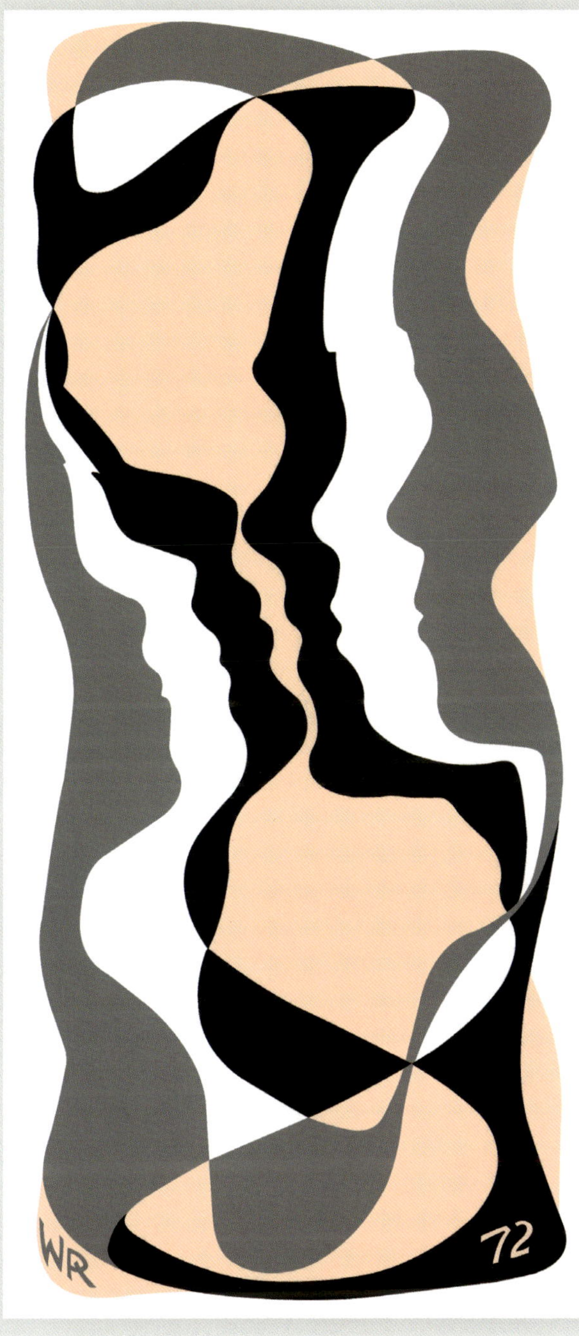
WR
72

GUITAR QUARTET
1973

Beginning in the mid-60s the guitar became preeminent in the world of contemporary music. In this card four guitars in a semi-abstract design proclaim the advent of Christmas.

The fairly complicated color scheme is achieved by the overprinting of four of the five separate screens.

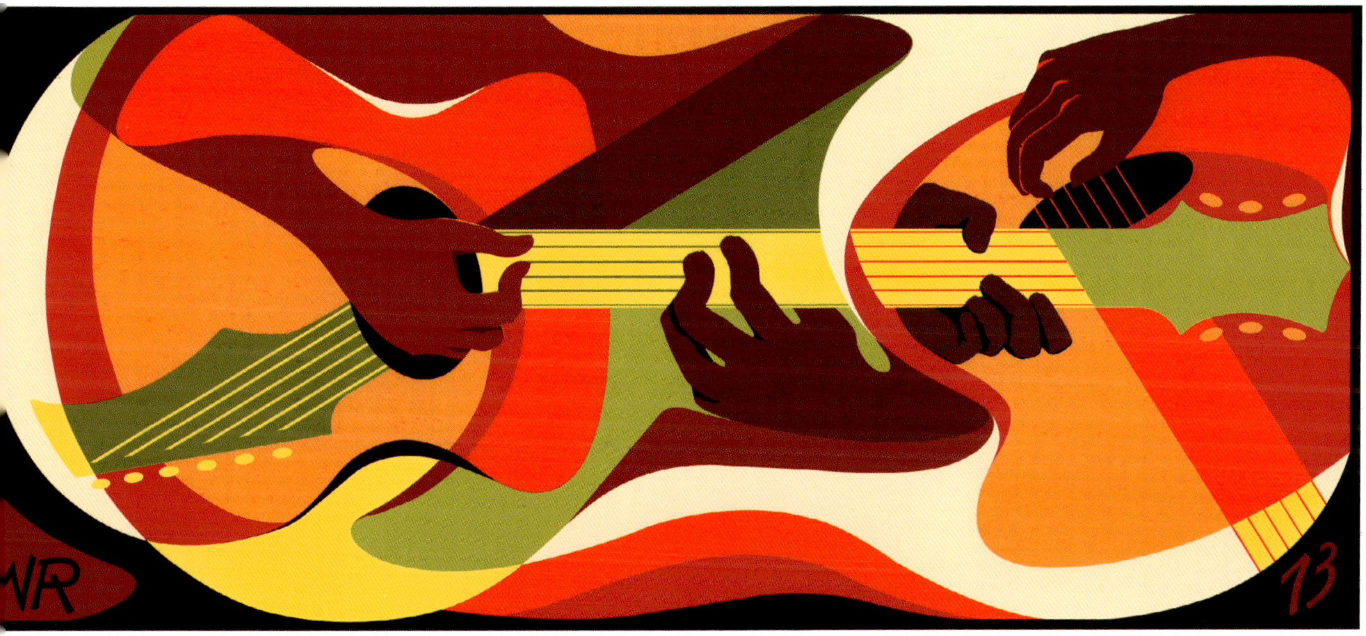

PAX
1974

Despite the stabilizing effect in the 1970s of two balanced world powers, United States and the Soviet Union, the world was far from peaceful. Then as now, strife in the Middle East and the greed for oil were the main impediments to lasting world peace.

To me, even a minor art like a Christmas card was a possible medium through which to express the widespread hope for peace.

Once again, as with the 1967 “hands/Noel” design on p 45, I have attempted to blend imagery with text. Perhaps the device of placing conventional doves of peace over the word *PAX* was somewhat blunt, but at least the message was clear. Overprinting of the three inks, ultramarine blue, cyan, and magenta, produced the rich purple and the grey-blue.

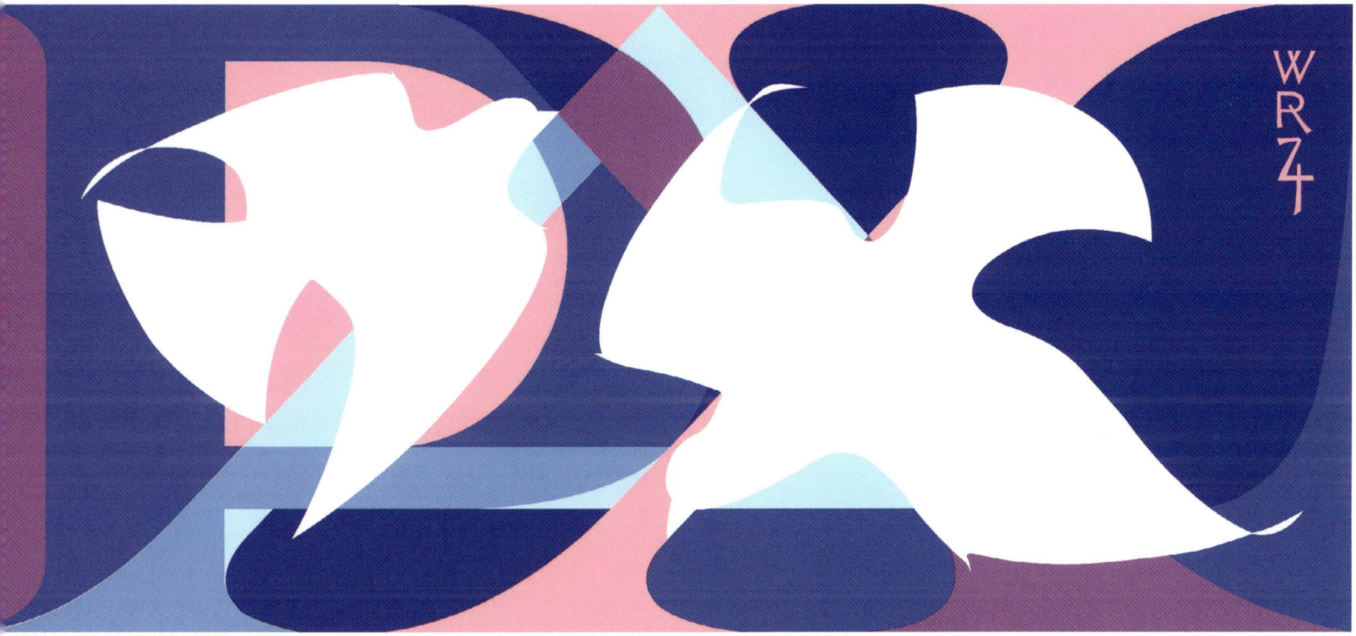

HELPING HANDS
1975

Again, as with the 1967 card on p 45, human hands were the subject, this time to express the need for more interracial co-operation, tolerance and aid for developing countries.

Although the subject is perhaps overly detailed, the impact of the design is saved by a simple, two-screen printing sequence of just black and vermilion.

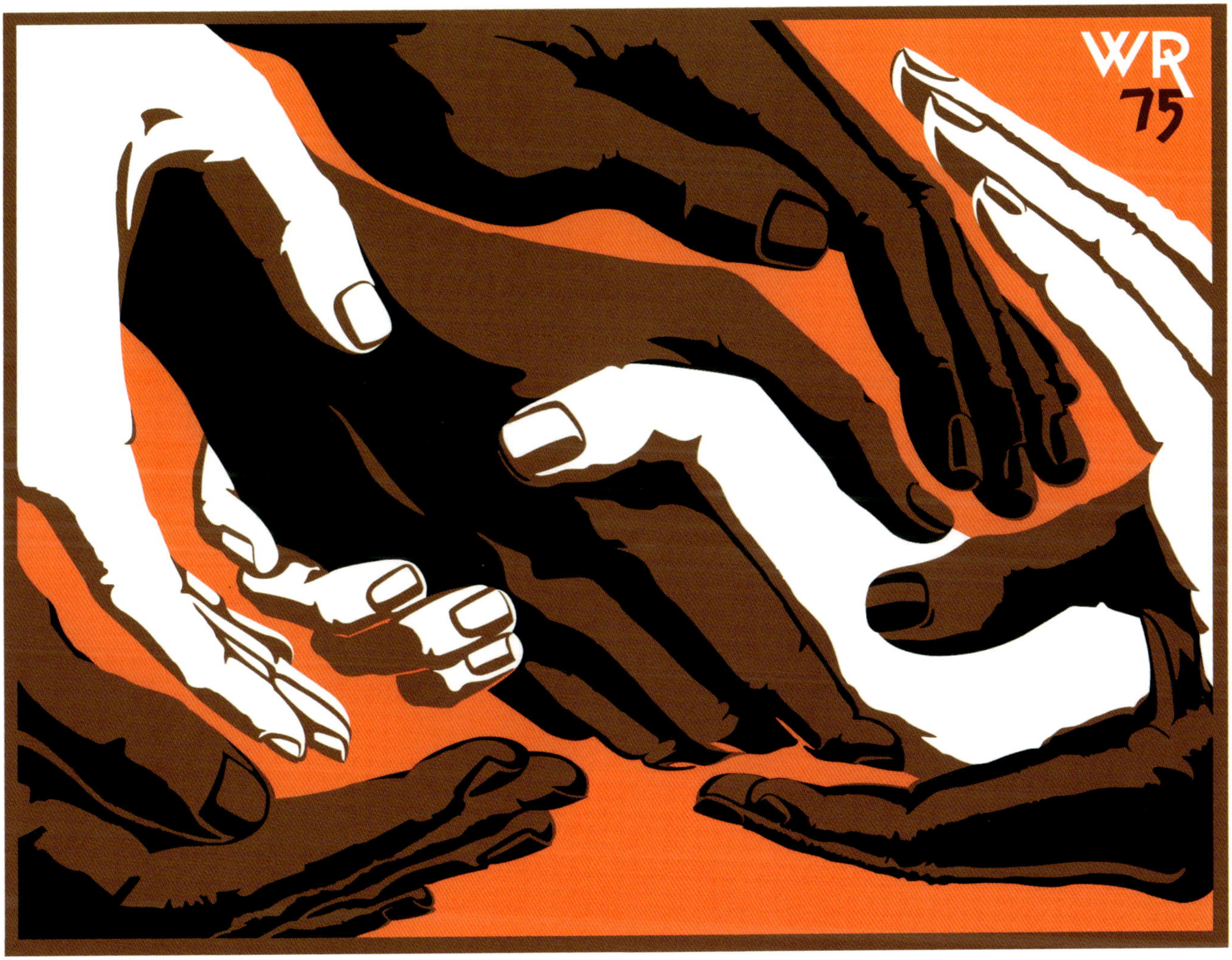
WR
75

PROST!
1976

For any celebration such as a wedding, an anniversary or Christmas, Heidi's parents, both German immigrants, would often propose this toast in the European style. We decided to share their happy gesture in the design of this Christmas card for 1976.

Much later, in 1990, my sons, Robin and Ryan, both asked me to duplicate the same design for their wedding invitation cards. The guests at both weddings seemed to appreciate the break from the traditional colorless, white embossed invitations.

I used only three screens: chocolate brown, tan, and vermilion. Two overprints produced the other earth tones necessary for the design.

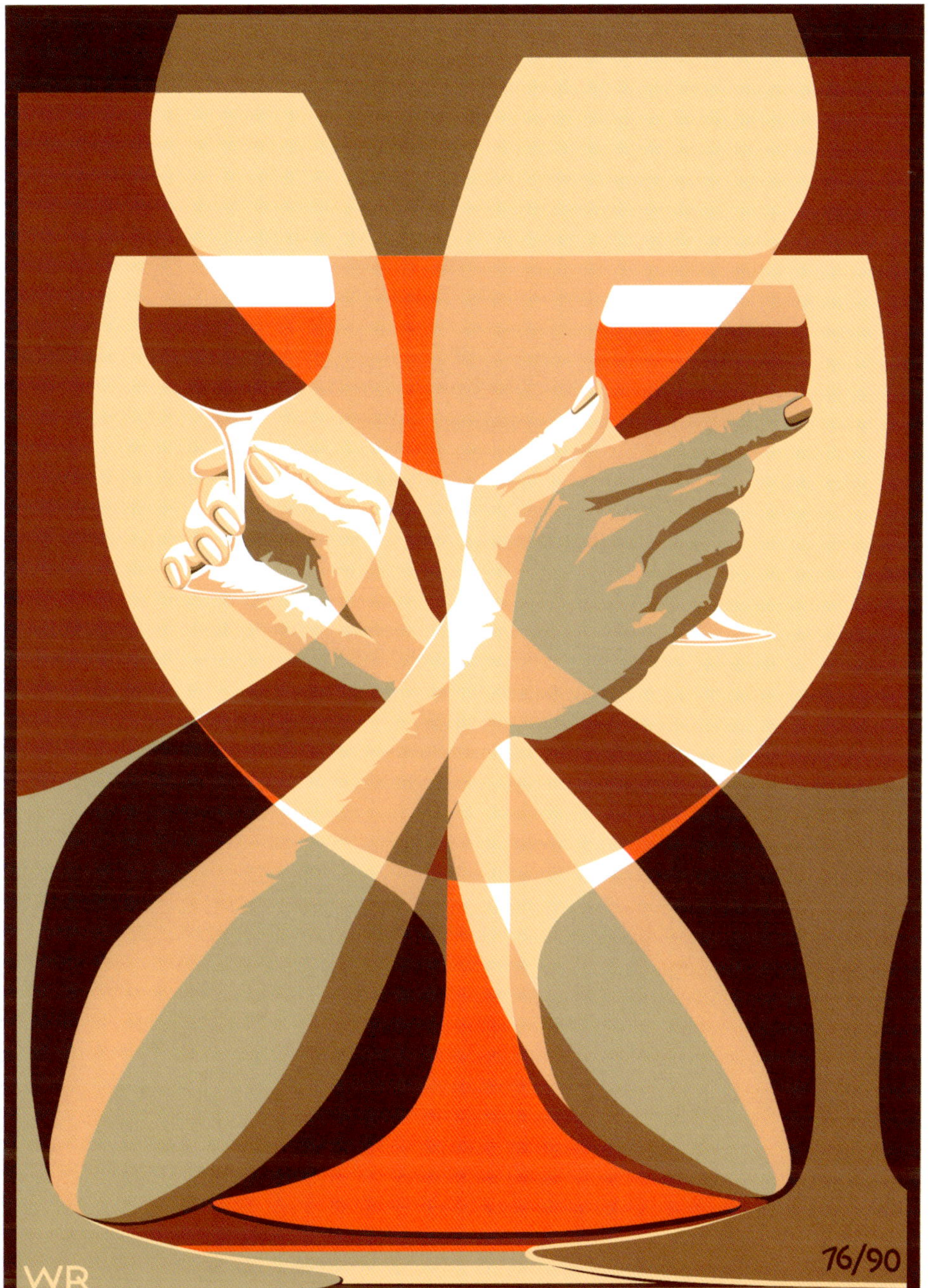
WR
76/90

NORTHERN PINE
1977

The tree was from a sketch made years ago of a shaggy old pine behind one of the schools on Canadian Forces Base Cold Lake, Alberta. I thought it would make an interesting centre of interest for a card commemorating our family's many visits to nearby Pierce Lake, Saskatchewan. I "transplanted" the tree, simplified and stylized, to stand on the south shore of this lake. The sky recalls an actual evening spent around a campfire there; a threatening thunder storm suddenly dissipated and the sky broke into vibrant bands of rose and purple.

This print required four screens: black, violet, magenta, and a semi-opaque flesh color. Overprinting produced the salmon, warm grey, and deep purple.

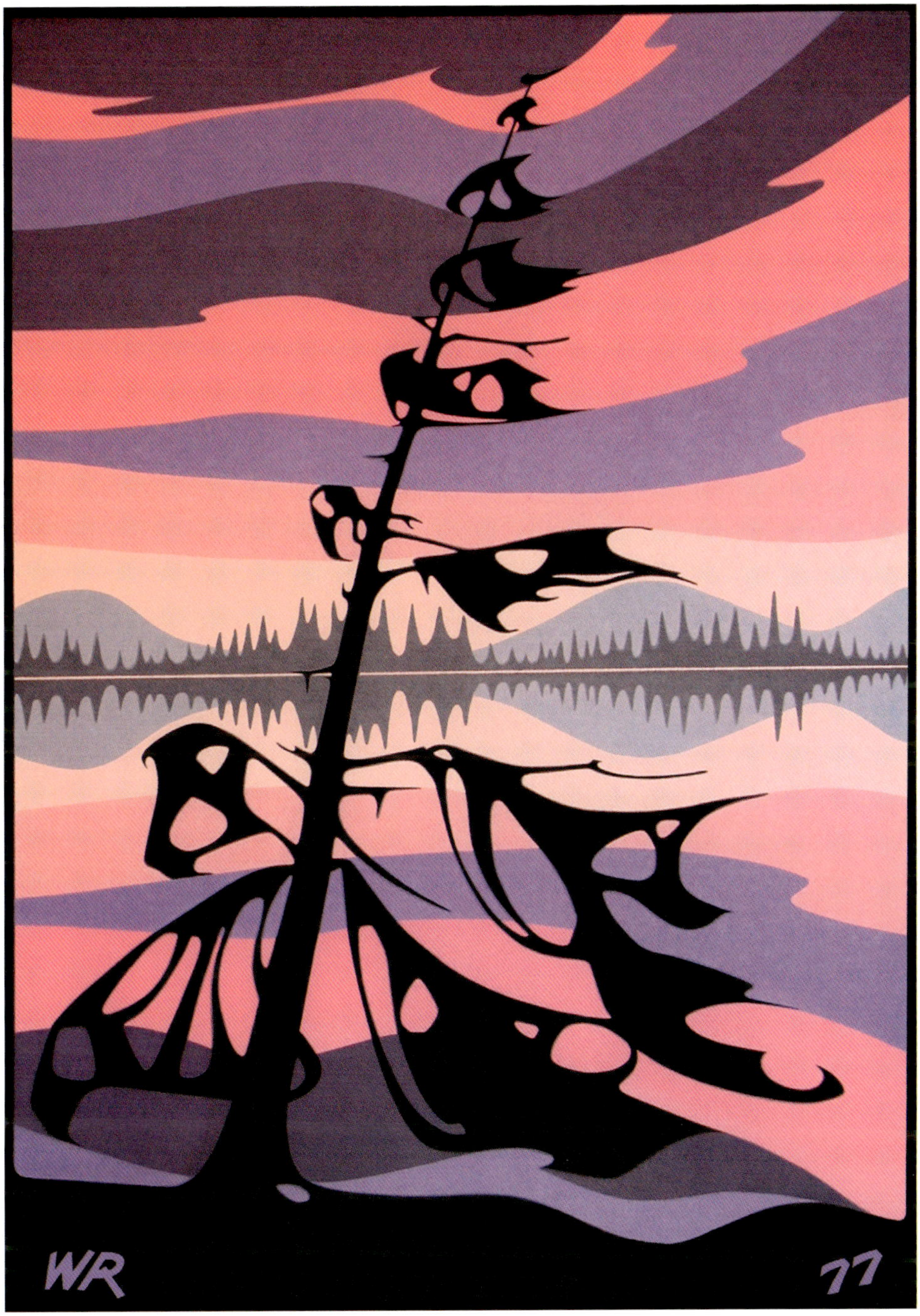
WR
77

ALBERTA ROSE
1978

At this point I decided to embark on a series of Christmas cards featuring the floral emblems of the various provinces. The idea persisted for only one year, as on reconsideration I thought that the series could become rather "blah" and repetitious.

The screening for this floral design involved four inks: "navy", rose, yellow, and a semi-transparent white. Overprinting produced an olive green, a light green, pink, orange, and lemon yellow.

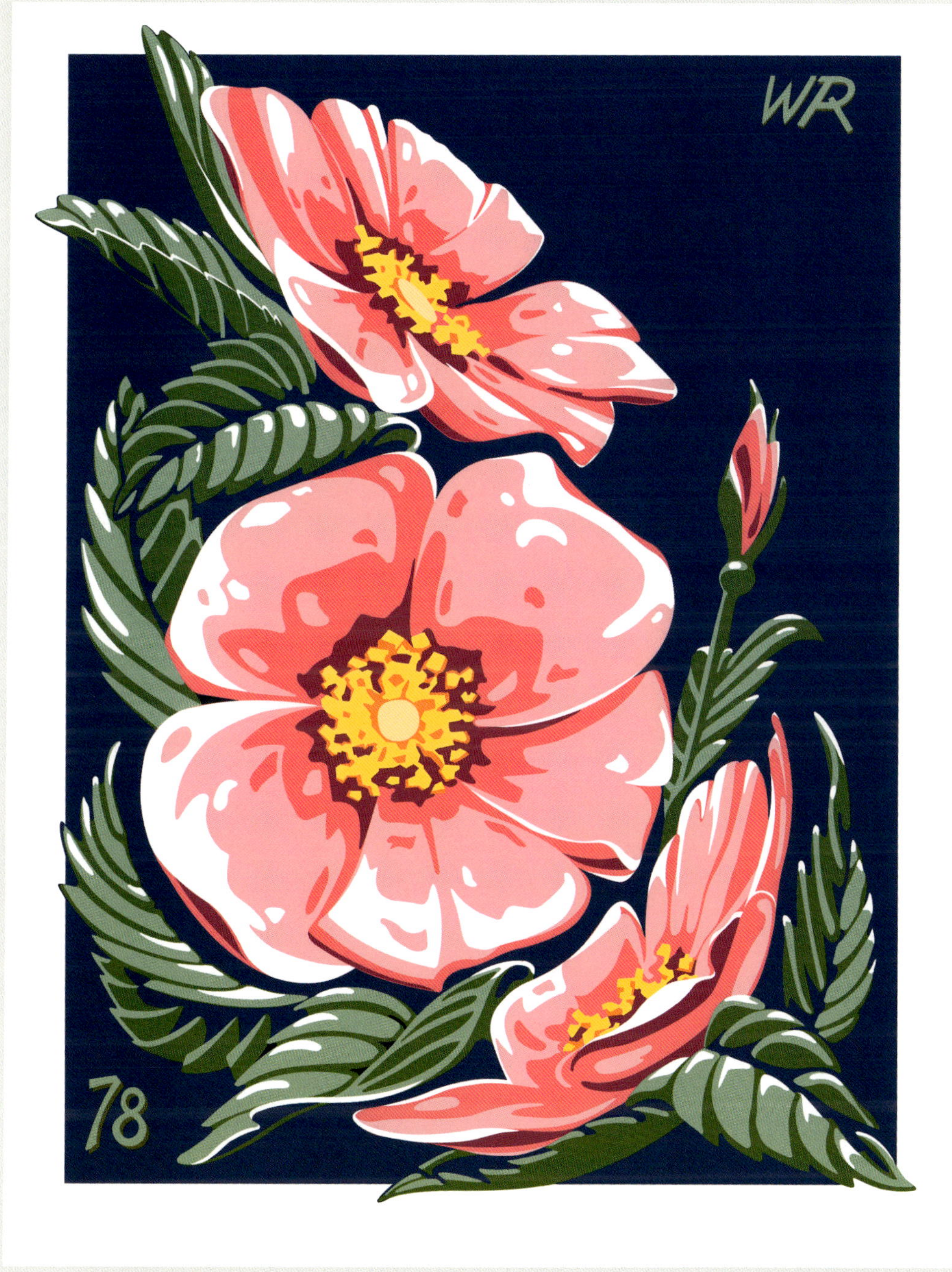
WR
78

WORLD RELIGIONS
1980

By the 1980s immigration, travel and renewed tolerance had begun to change the western world. No longer, at Christmas, could we think solely of our own Christian faith. The adopting of a new, generous spirit of ecumenism had emerged. We were learning to appreciate religions and cultures other than our own.

This simple design is an attempt to show the unity among all religions by combining the symbols of several great world faiths: Christianity, Hinduism, Islam, Judaism, and Buddhism. Many of the less universal but equally important religions were not included, such as the indigenous North American religions and other important Asian faiths such as Sikhism, Shintoism and Jainism.

Like the design, the color scheme was also quite simple, involving only three screens: ultramarine blue, light cyan, and chartreuse. Overprinting produced green and blue-grey.

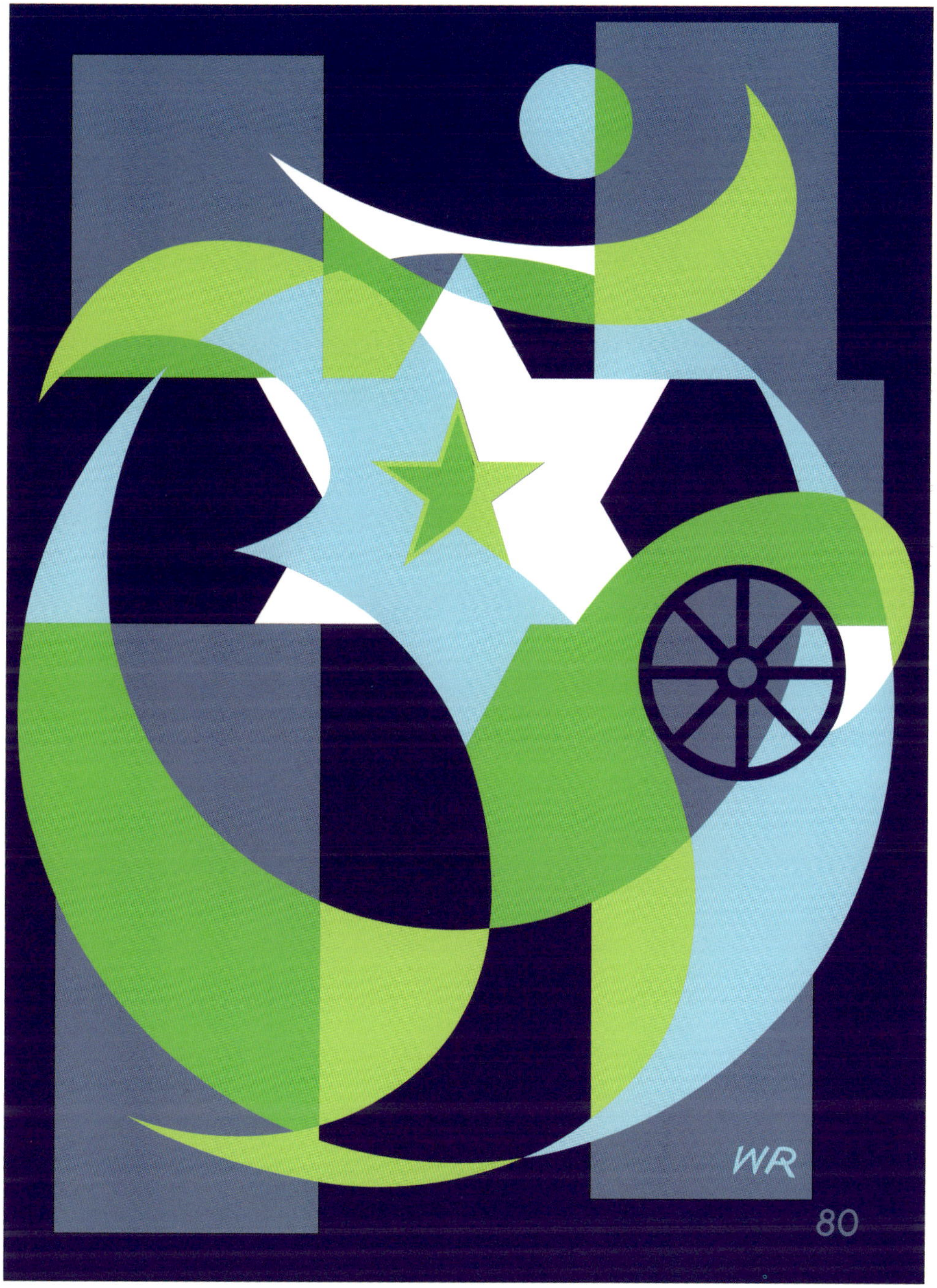
WR
80

GRAIN ELEVATORS
1981

In 1980 my wife, Heidi, and I had a memorable holiday in Saskatchewan. On our way home, somewhere near Macklin, we spotted a pair of elevators standing alone in the middle of wheat fields. Seeing them, I recalled another pair of elevators etched strongly in my memory—the old *Pool* and *Western* in the hamlet of Tullis, Saskatchewan, where I was raised. (See p 88.) We took time to walk into the fields so that we could watch the hot, harvest sun set between the elevators. The pattern of swathed grain is from another sketch made near the town of Vermilion in Alberta.

The fairly complicated color scheme involved five screens with overprinting producing a total of 16 colors. This particular color arrangement is treated in some detail in the introduction to these serigraph Christmas cards on p 37.

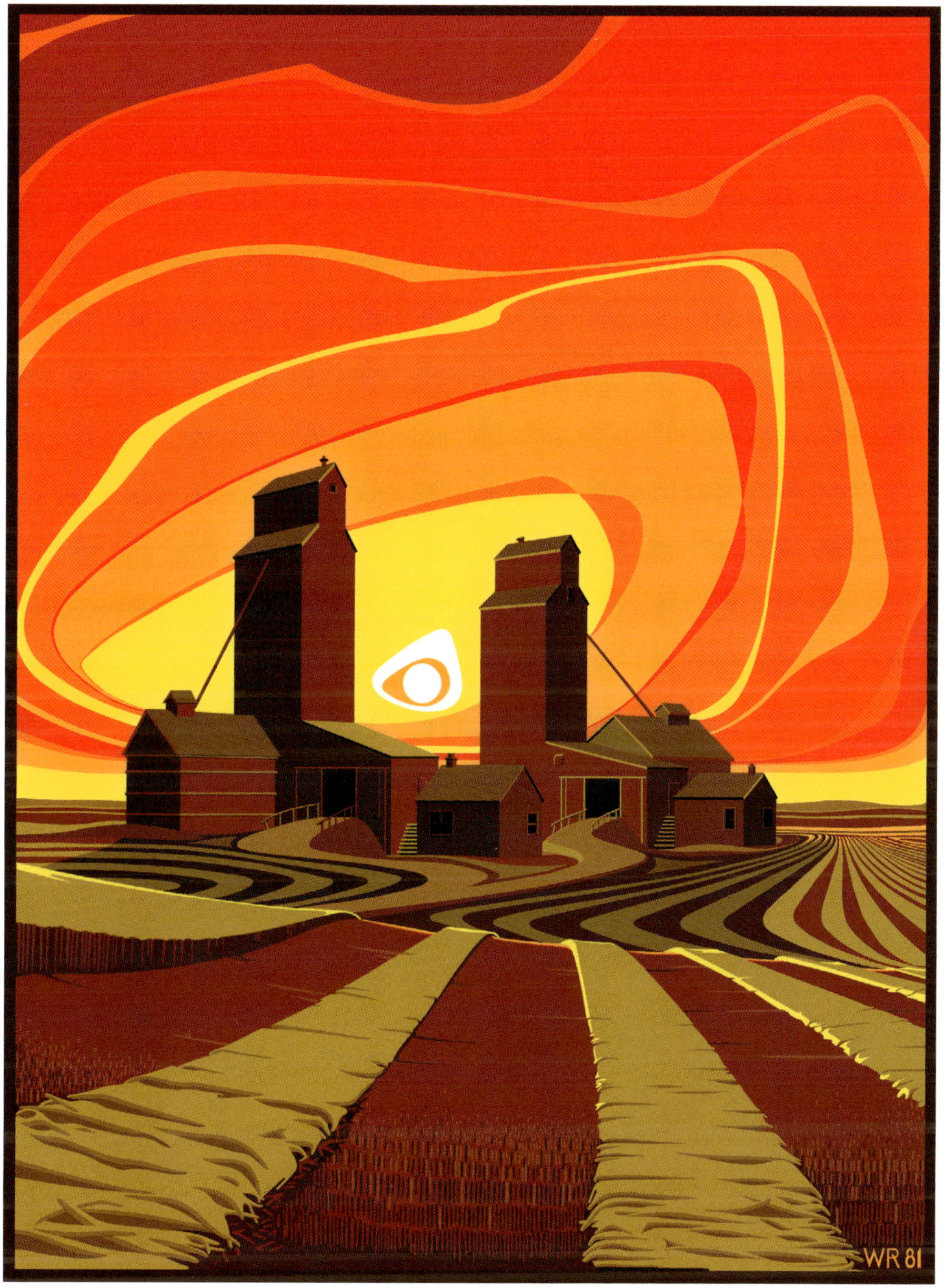
WR 81

CANDELABRUM
1982

Over the years I had always eschewed "Christmas candles" as a topic, but in 1982 I decided to design an abstract candelabrum to express the festive spirit of Christmastime.

As usual, all four screens for this design were done with hand-cut lacquer stencils, but with one innovation. The gradations for the tops of the candle flames and the candle body shading were done with various sized hypodermic needles (ground as punches) to make tiny holes in the stencils. The four inks used were black, violet, dark cyan, and yellow. Secondary colors produced by overprinting were lime, olive green, dark olive green, and ultramarine blue.

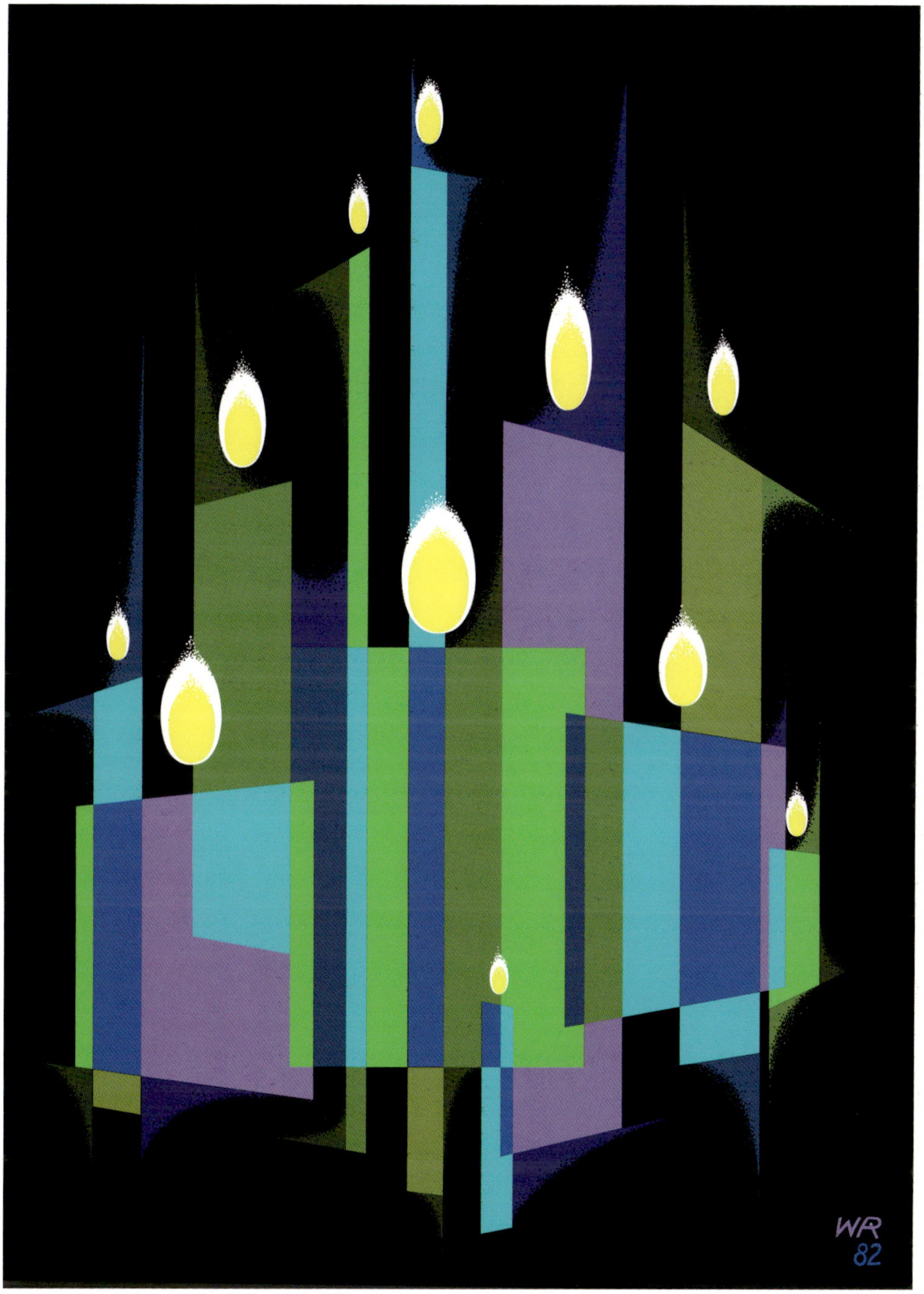
WR
82

RETIRED!
1983

In June, 1984, I finally retired as principal of one of the schools on Canadian Forces Base Cold Lake. The exiguous male figure breaking through the binding chains of the workaday world is yours truly. The exaggerated stance of this central figure was intended to be a light-hearted, perhaps comical expression of the near ecstasy some of us feel upon retiring!

The monotone color scheme of this print was achieved by overprinting three screens of varying flesh colors.

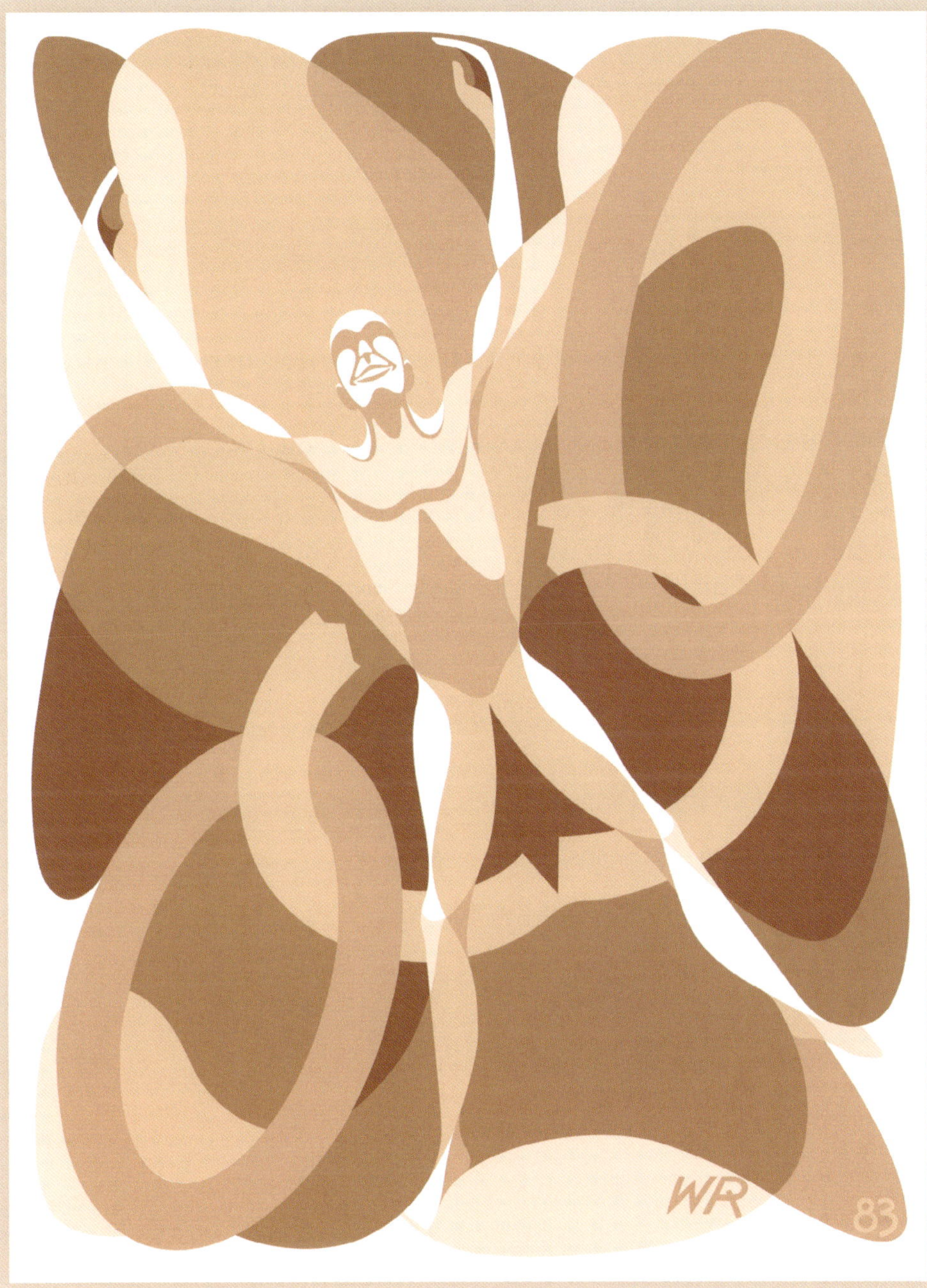
WR
83

CAROL OF THE BELLS
1984

This simple design of six transparent, stylized and overlapping bells was inspired by the Ukrainian Yuletide hymn, “Carol of the Bells”, which has always been a favorite of mine.

The effects of overprinting the grey, red, and blue bell shapes are quite uncomplicated. Again, as with *Candelabrum* on p 73, hypodermic needle punches were used to make the “sound shadows” around the bells.

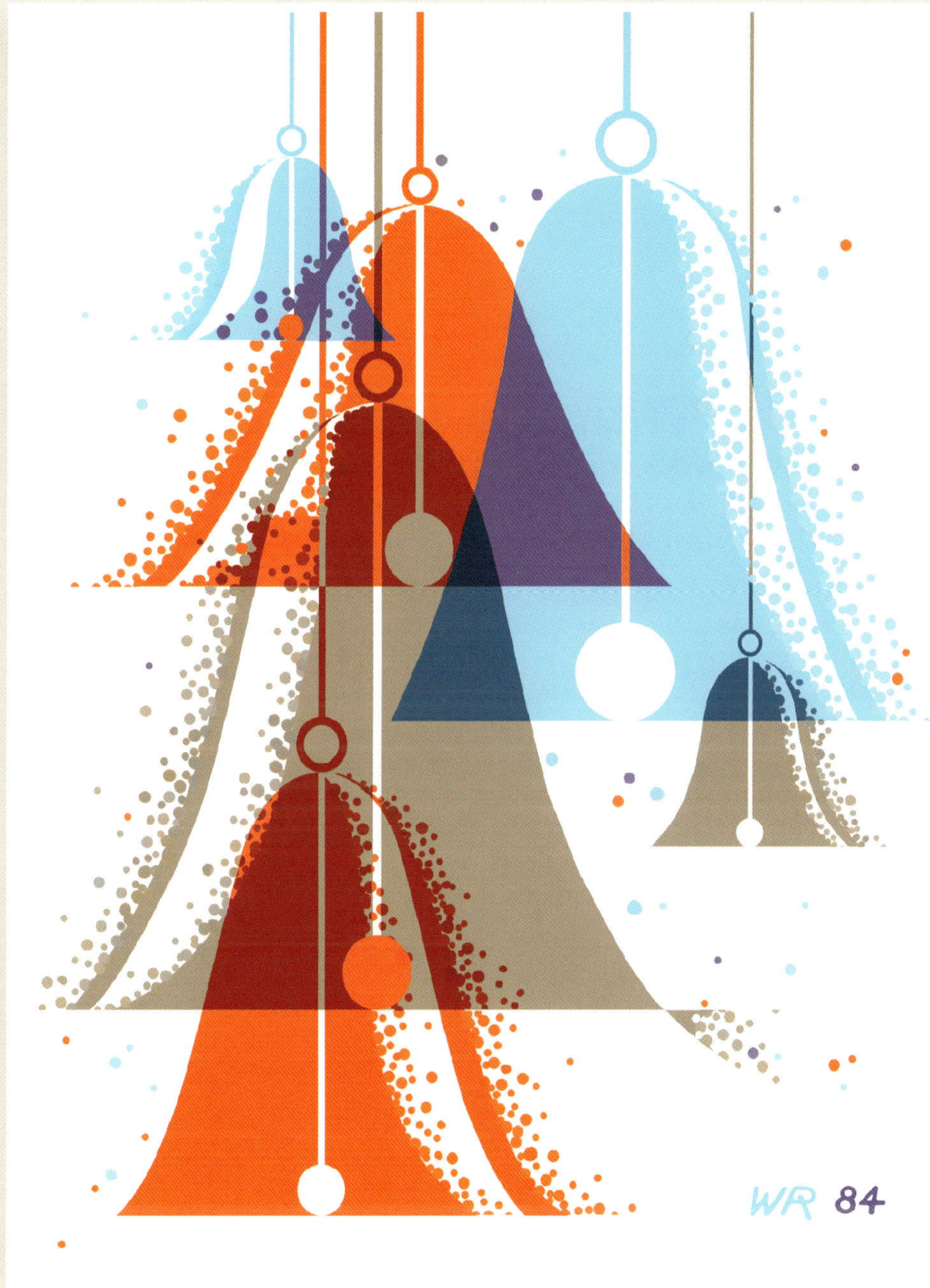
WR 84

YULE FIRE
1985

Yule Fire was my attempt to symbolize the warmth and hospitality which the Yule fire has brought to countless generations during the bleakest days of winter. It also, recalls our boyhood when my brother Frank and I would rush to the farmhouse windows on Saskatchewan winter mornings to see who could find the best leaf patterns in the thick frost before the heat from our own fires would melt clear, watery holes in the middle of each delicate frost design.

The "white-on-white" frost part of the design required two screens, white and a light, opaque grey printed on a deeper grey colored paper. The stylized fire required three more screens: yellow, vermilion, and dark blue, overprinted to produce the two shades of orange and the browns for the logs.

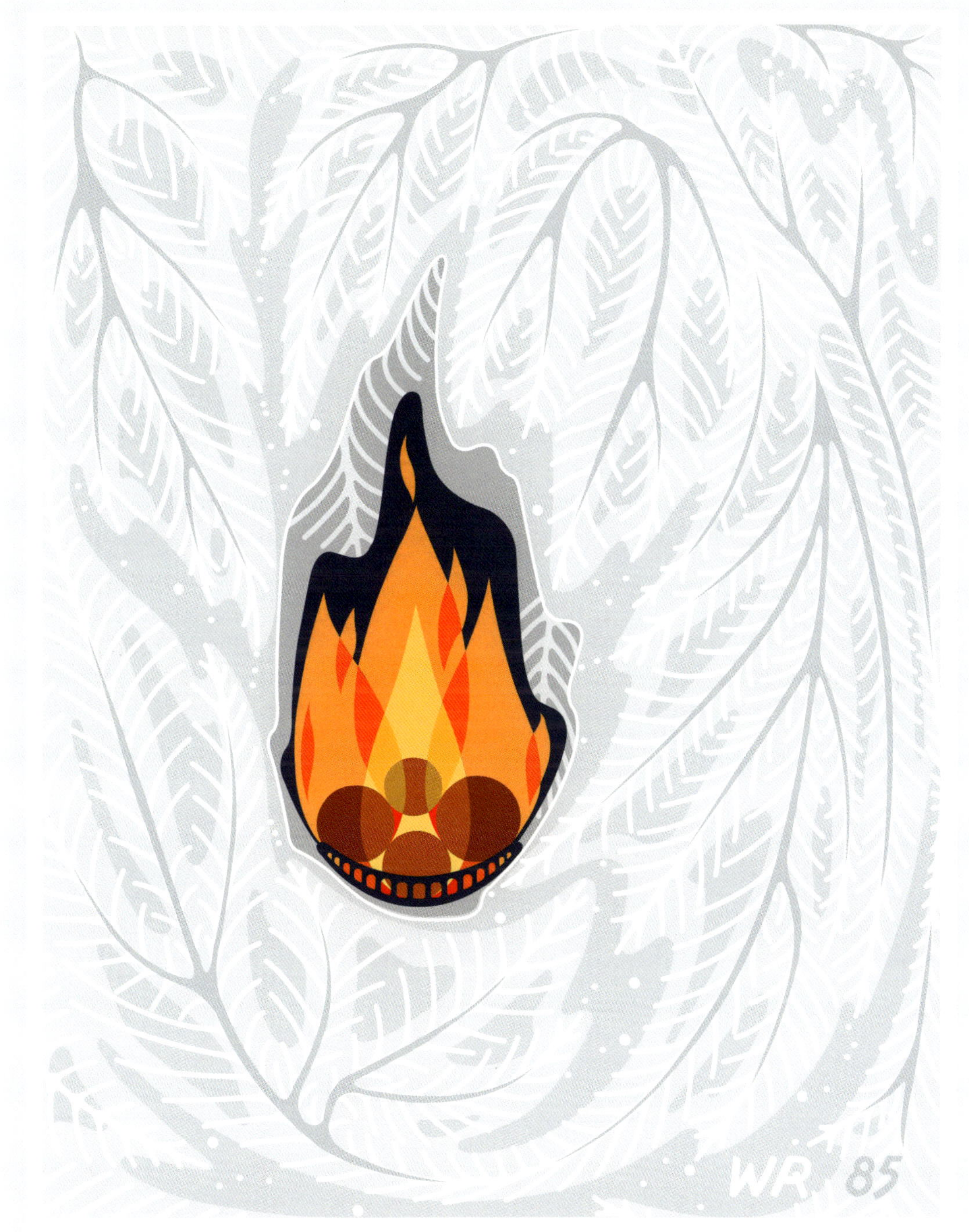
WR 85

STAINED GLASS FOREST
1986

Twenty years previously, in 1966, we called our Christmas card *Autumn Forest.* (See p 43) After all those years I was still fascinated by the magic that the fall season brought to the "bush country". Then as now, if you looked into the forest against a low sun, the gold poplars and the red high-bush cranberry bushes seemed transparent, their conical, almost leaf-like shapes overlapping one against the other. Their near fluorescence was enhanced by the black-green irregularity of the pines or spruce among them. Everywhere you looked were thousands of stained glass windows!

In this fairly complicated design, four inks, black, red, yellow and teal were over-printed to produce the various shades of brown, green and orange.

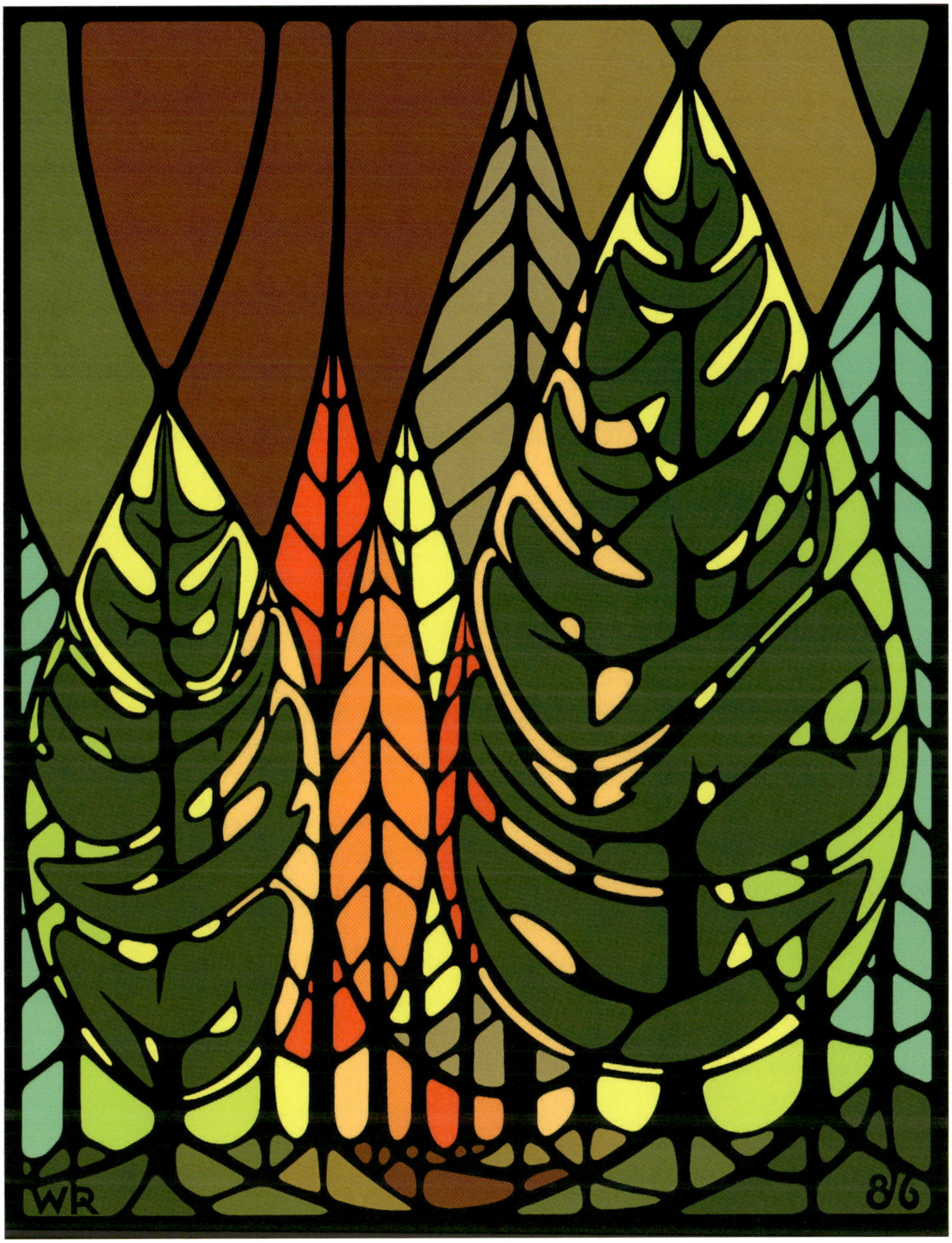
WR
8/6

NORTHERN LIGHTS
1987

One advantage to living north of the fifty-fourth parallel for so many years was our frequent opportunities to witness nature's greatest "free show"—the northern lights. It is hard to believe that these dramatic, waving curtains of light are usually about 80 kilometres above our heads and that they are often over 50 kilometres tall. Thirty-one years before, in 1956, I chose the northern lights—same topic and same title—for a simple linocut Christmas card that year. (See p 27.) Preceding the 1987 serigraph, I had produced three large oil paintings of the northern lights. One of them was successful.

In all renderings of this topic over a period of the thirty-one years, I tried to express the sheer dominance of these dynamic light displays over the landscape below. The ever-changing colors from pale green and lime to brilliant pinks, and the swift, rippling undulations are almost beyond the scope of any static art.

Techniques involved in the production of this serigraph were quite complex: To begin with, the main part of the design was realized with three regular, hand-cut lacquer stencils to print light turquoise, ultramarine blue and dark blue. Overprinting in various combinations produced the variety of blues required. The variegated colors of the northern lights and parts of the snowdrifts were achieved entirely with two separate "squeegee blends" made through a fourth stencil. Although this procedure was carefully controlled, there was some variation from one print to the next. I first attempted this technique in the 1965 card, *Forty Below* on p 41. Shading on the snow banks and the conical shapes of the trees was achieved using the same hypodermic needle punches employed in *Candelabrum*, 1982, on p 73 and in *Carol of the Bells*, 1984, on p 77.

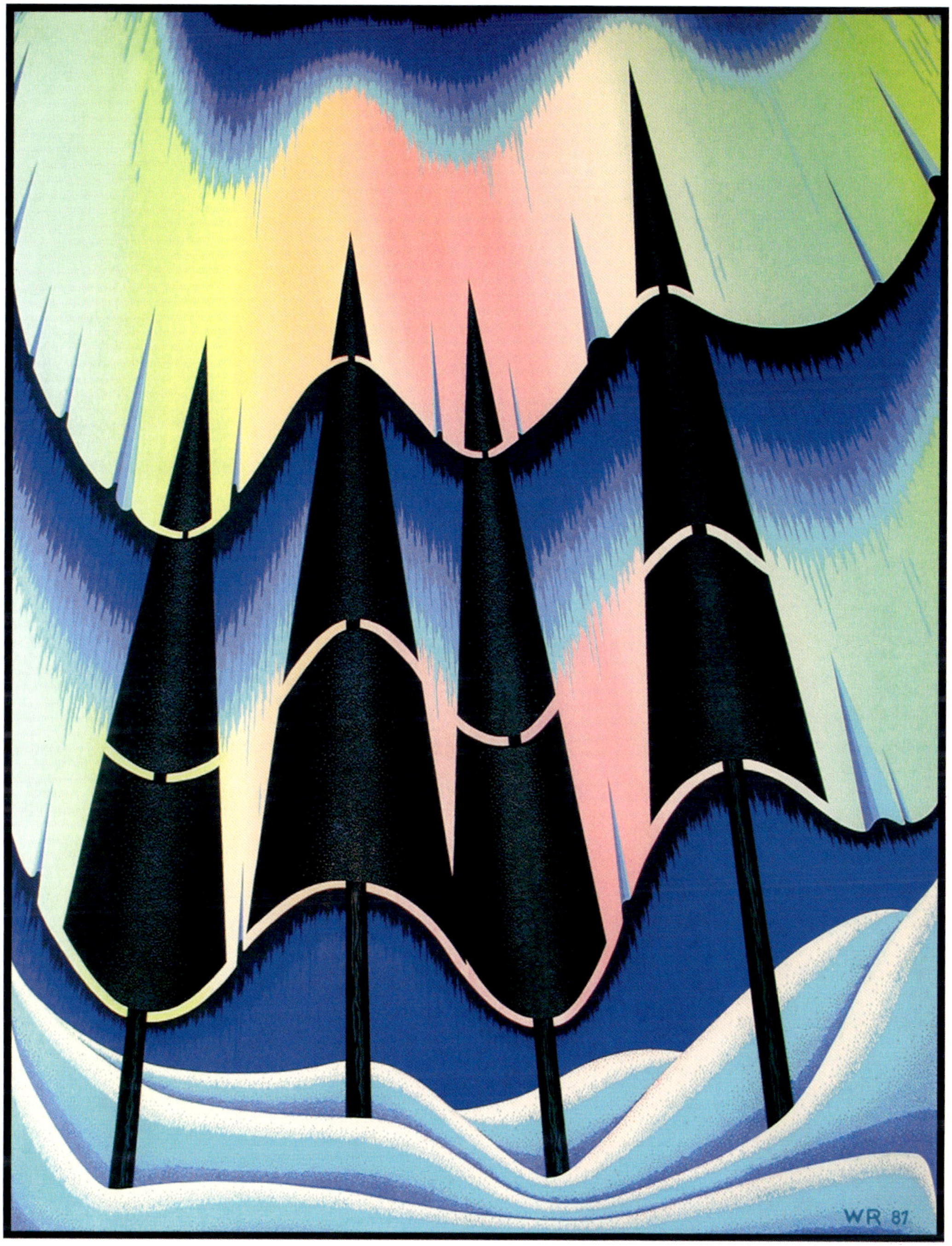
WR 87

HEAVY OIL
1988

Now beginning a fourth decade of steady development, the heavy oil industry has become an important part of the socio-economic structure of the Cold Lake area in Alberta. The current steam injection technology, the costly kilometers of elevated, insulated pipelines, and the jumbo-sized pumps make heavy oil an extremely capital-intensive process—at the mercy of world oil prices. After riding out several economic crises, the industry is currently in a solid financial position.

Some of the “satellite pads” (clusters of pumps) are installed with remarkably little disruption of the natural beauty surrounding them. This print is a composite design based on the observations of a number of installations, and does not represent a particular site. Also, considerable “artistic licence” was taken with this design. The pumps operate in a quite random way, but here they are stopped at 45° rotational intervals so that the curved outline of the jacks would harmonize with the hills in the background. The elevated pipes are usually behind the satellite pads but I wanted to show them in front as part of the design.

This card required six stencils with the following printing sequence: black, cerulean blue, orange, transparent white, opaque white, and a correction black.

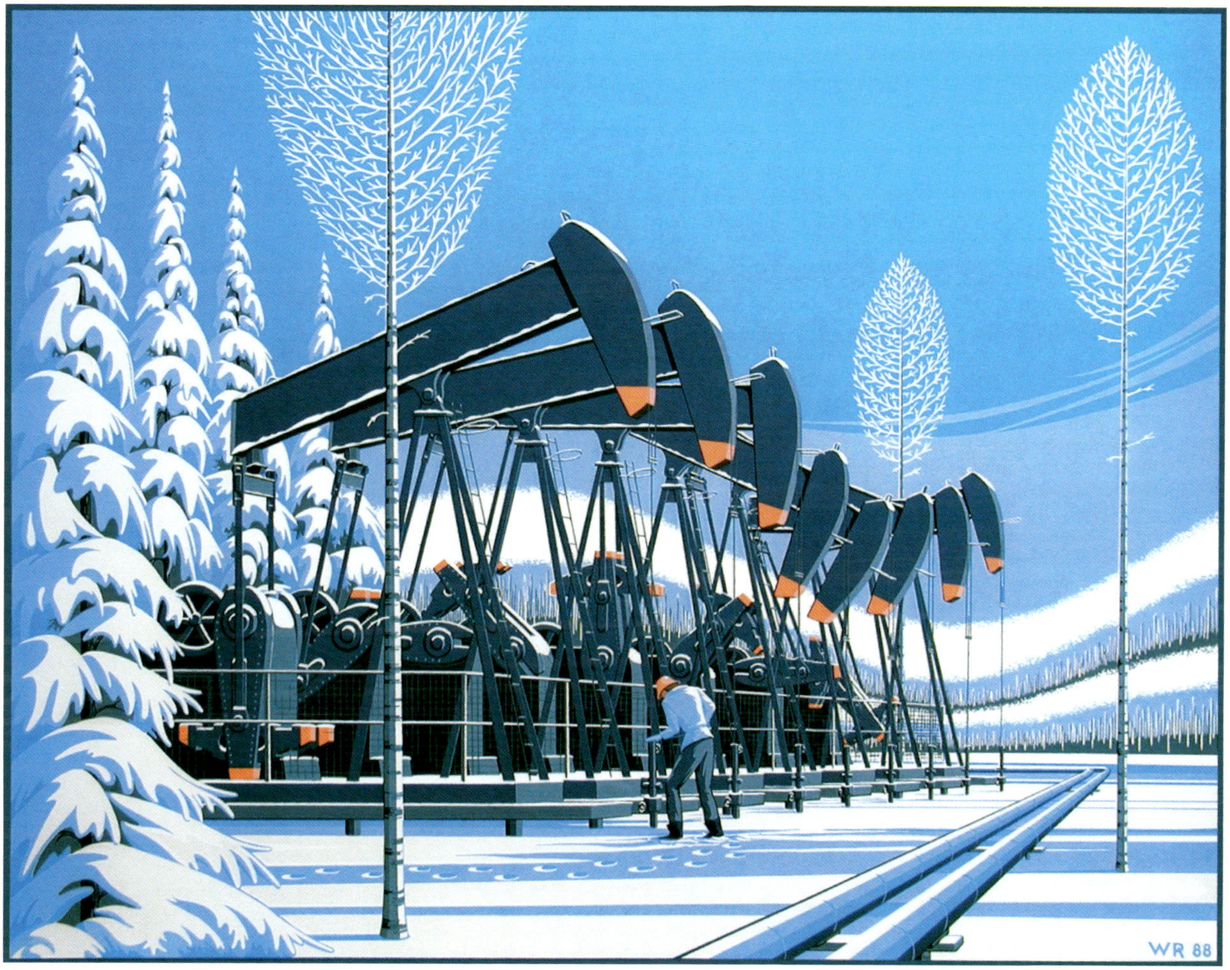
WR 88

YIN AND YANG
1990

About a thousand years before the first Christmas, the influential and far-reaching idea of **yin** and **yang** began take form in China and Japan. To believers, **yin** and **yang** are the two basic opposing principles which together a the substance of all creation. The negative **yin** is conceived to be the passive, dark, cool, moist energy associat with the earth and femininity. The positive **yang** is the active, light, warm and dry energy associated with t heavens and masculinity.

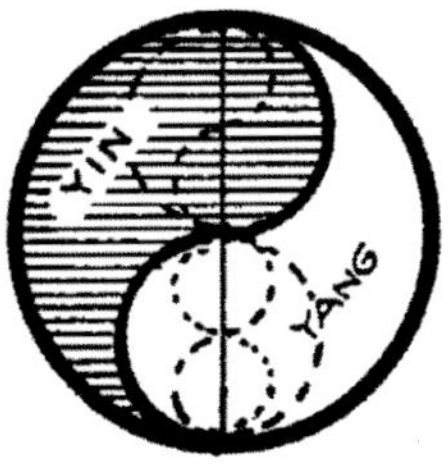

The traditional Chinese diagram (left) is a circle divided equally by a curving line whi winds gradually into the circumference line. As can be seen in the diagram, the separati line is formed by two opposing half circumferences of circles drawn within the big circ The length of this line, measured geometrically, is, surprisingly, exactly one-half of t circumference of the big circle! Therefore, the total length of either the **yin** or the **ya** outlines taken separately is equal to the total length of the big circle circumference.

In reference to the dotted outlines in the diagram, it is obvious that further dividing circles can be drawn to ma ever decreasing curving lines dividing smaller and smaller basic circles, carrying on and on infinitely to invisible speck.

The essential message of this diagram is an expression of the mystery of one circumference becoming two continuously—to show the "ten thousand things" in creation. The **yin** and **yang** are never really separate, a neither can ever be judged morally as good or evil, or in any way superior to the other. The **yin** and **yang** a believed to be present in all things animate and inanimate in a perpetual interaction which is, itself, the **Tao** eternal "law" of creation. One or the other is usually uppermost. In woman, for example, the **yin** usually predor nates, in man the **yang**; yet each are in both.

After the 5th century B.C. both the Confucian and Taoist philosophers began to stress the importance of a harn nious relationship of **yin** and **yang**. Rebellions, plagues and even floods were said to be caused by disruptions this harmony.

I have taken considerable licence in this **Yin** and **Yang** design: First, I chose the ellipse rather than the traditio circle to represent the idea of unity. To me the egg-shape helps to connote the idea of genesis. The "gene streams" of ovals are added for the purposes of design and also to symbolize the "ten thousand things" of creati To purists, perhaps my greatest liberty is the addition of Adam-and-Eve-like figures (with current North Americ conventions of "beauty" dominating!). This aspect of the design is more in the East Indian tradition where the t basic forces are more anthropomorphic and less abstract.

Only two screens were used for this print, the color gradations all achieved with "squeegee blends".

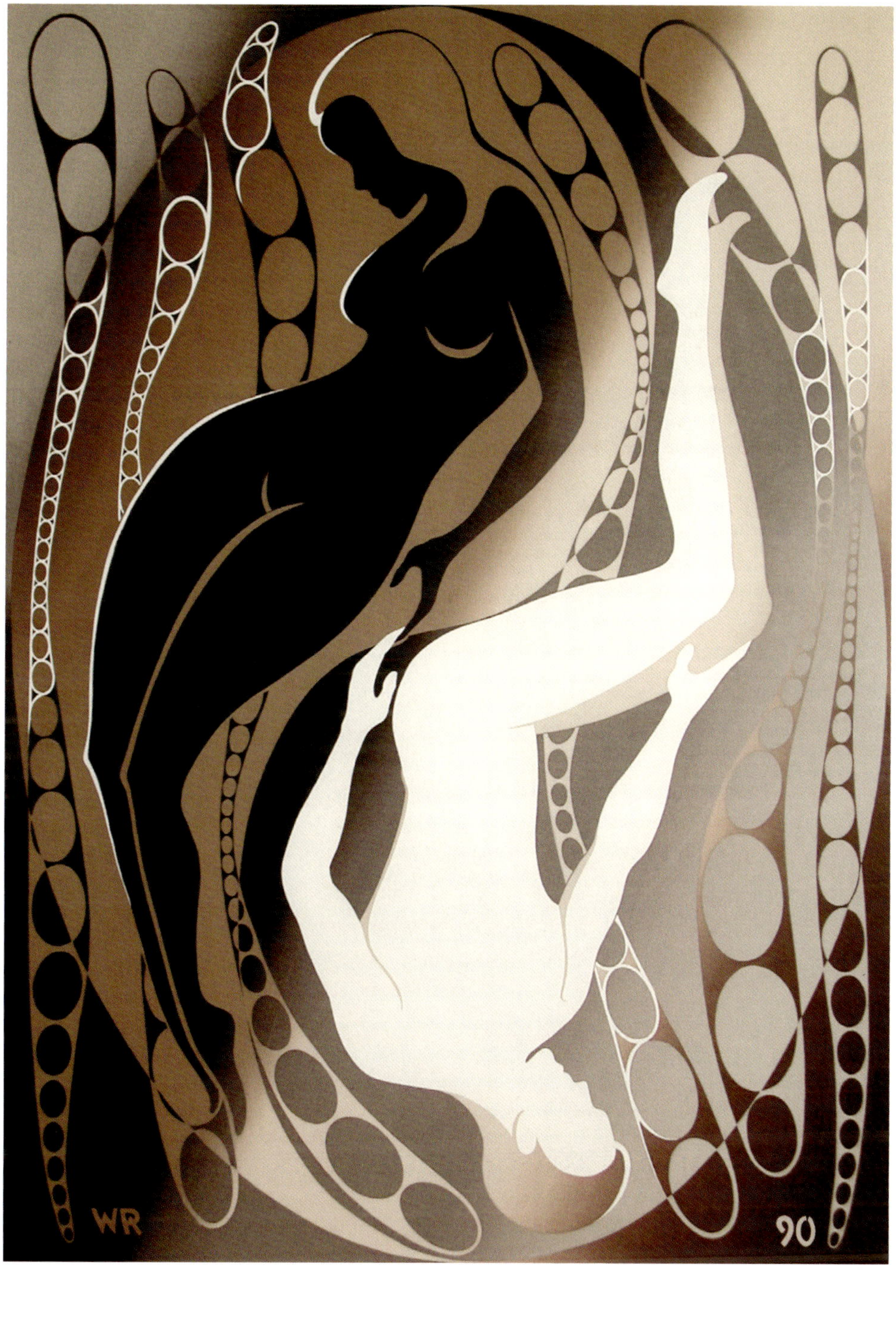
WR
90

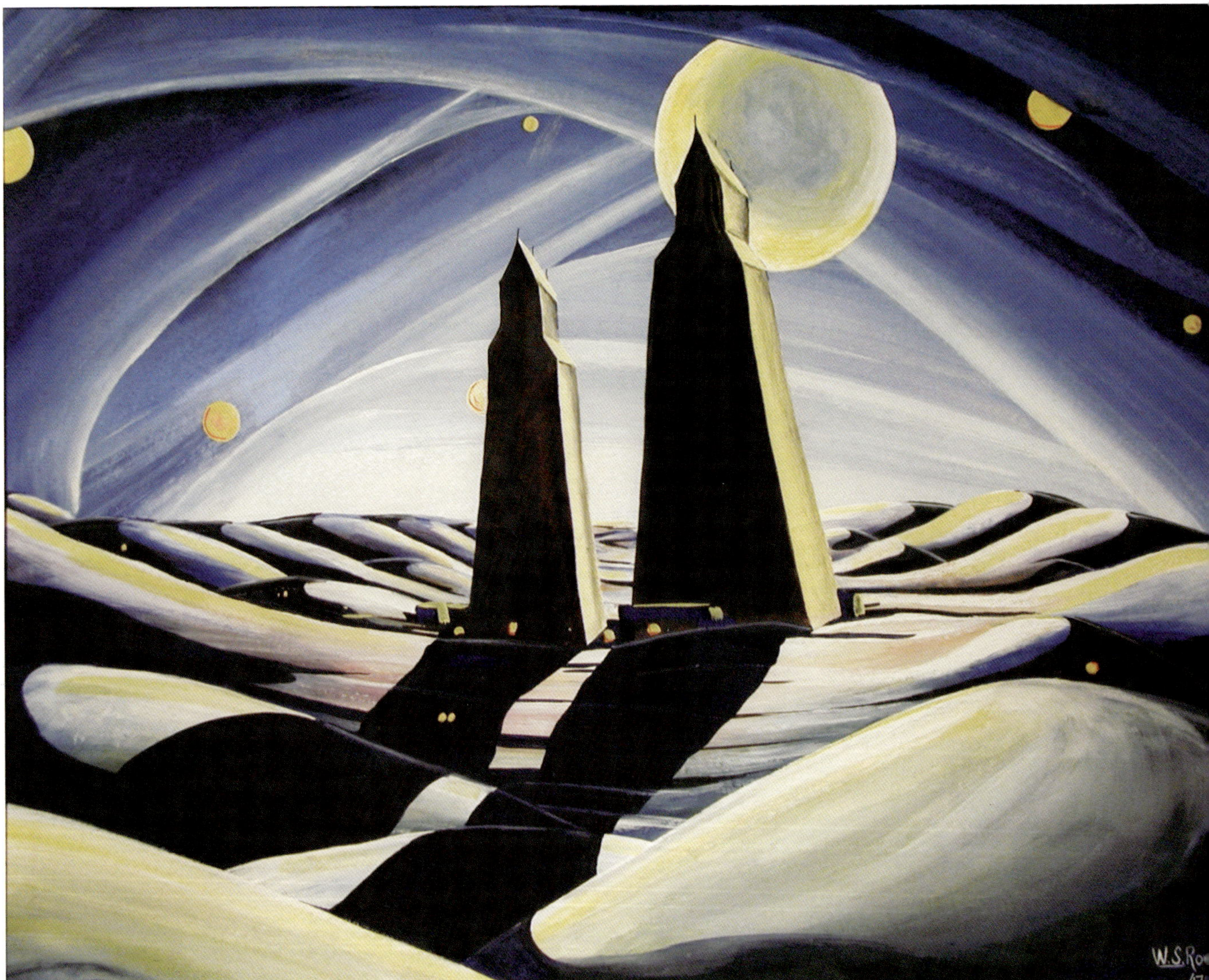

Prairie Sentinels 1947, tempera, 32.8 x 42.8 cm

THE CHRISTMAS CARDS FEATURING REPRODUCTIONS

The nine cards illustrated and described on pp 90 – 107 all featured reproductions of various original works which we wanted to share with our friends at Christmas time. Some of the pieces chosen for reproduction were current; some were three or four decades old. The sequence was random—for example, with the "English Bay series" of paintings, #2 was used first in 1994; #1 was not chosen until 1997. (See dated summary on p 120.)

The selections for the cards comprise a variety of media including pen-and-ink, oil and acrylic. Subject matter also is quite varied, but with some repetition and a fairly consistent philosophy. As mentioned elsewhere, I have tried to respect the advice of my mentor, the late Ernest Lindner, who always said that any subject worth doing once was worth doing twice. It was he who also said something to the effect that since the invention of the camera the purpose of art is not to record but to organize and to interpret. Although many of Lindner's paintings were "super realism", he never neglected design and interpretation!

As with most "Sunday painters" my work has not been extensive, but we do have a modest collection from which we made these nine choices—to provide a bit of variety and a change from graphic art alone.

HOARFROST
1989

Originally painted in 1969
Acrylic on wood panel
67 x 95 cm

This subject, repeated several times over the years in various media, is an impression of a favorite little snow-filled ravine alongside the access road to Canadian Forces Base Cold Lake, Alberta. On our way to work on many a winter day, Heidi and I enjoyed this bit of undefiled nature.

The technique, somewhat experimental, is one I would like to develop further (time permitting!). The acrylic paint was applied with brush, painting knife and large hypodermic syringe—over a heavy impasto of cellulose fibre dough.

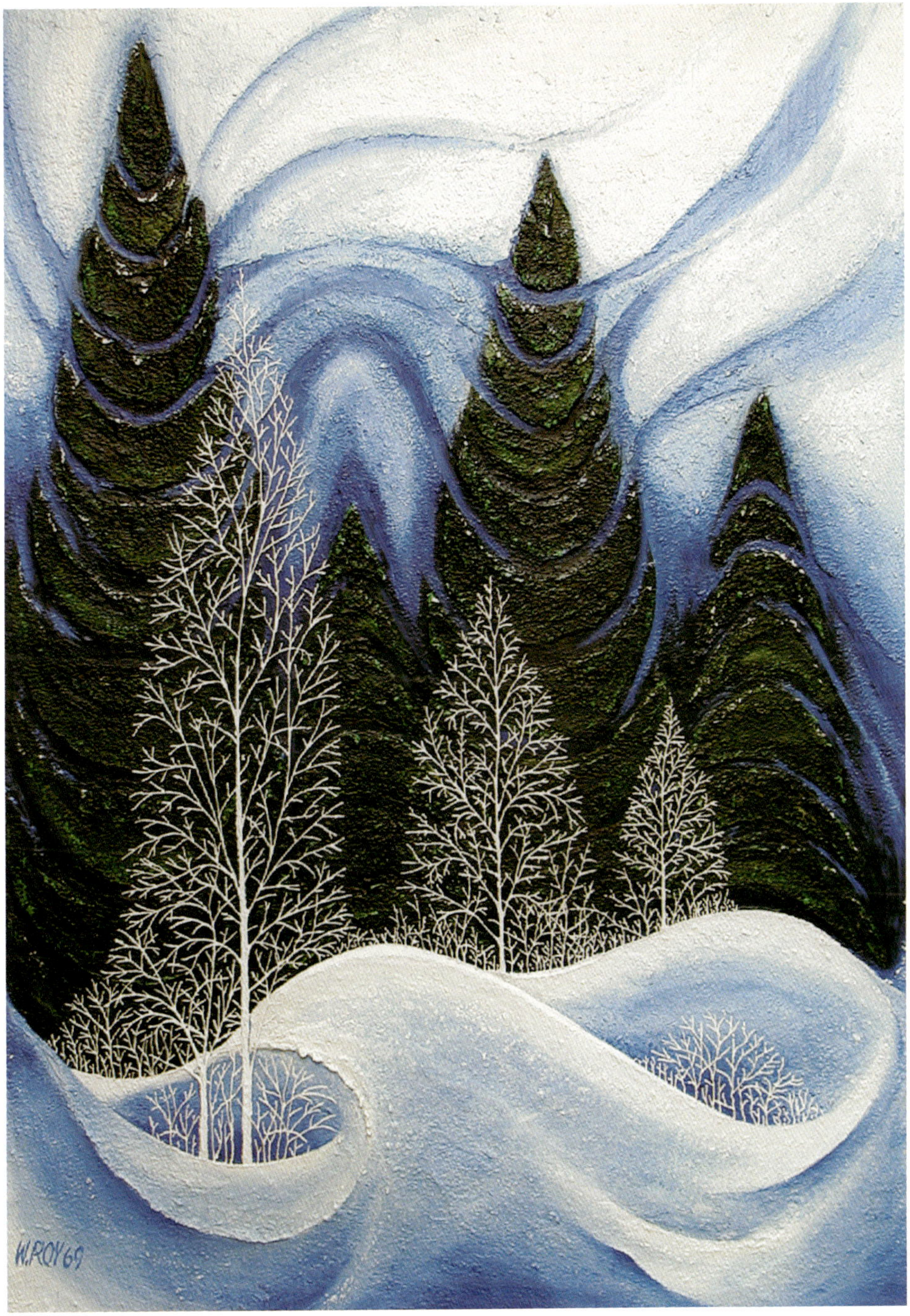
W.ROY 69

ROCKY MOUNTAIN SHEEP
1991

Originally drawn in 1949
Offset print of a pen-and-ink sketch
12.5 x 16.5 cm

This bighorn ram I sketched in pen and ink at the tender age of twenty. Perhaps typical of the young, would-be "artist"—I seem to have been more concerned with **recording** the symmetry and forms of nature than bothering with **interpreting** nature. In deference to my excellent art teachers at the time, though, I had already attempted several other larger, more interpretive works with some success.

The sketch, as I remember, was inspired by the several sightings of bighorn sheep I had made during trips back and forth through the Rockies from Vancouver to Saskatoon. This and several other similar sketches or small paintings were done as a pastime during my first, snow-bound winter boarding with the Obarianyk family at Grainland, Saskatchewan, where I began teaching. A little further into spring, still in the same "naturalistic" style, I painted the small watercolor, *Crocuses*, reproduced on p 108.

In July, 1991 at Waterton National Park, about forty-two years later, Heidi and I came across about twenty-five bighorn ewes and lambs—all nosing around the cars in a roadside parking space—licking the car fenders (for salt or other minerals?). Unlike the haughty, almost belligerent ram in my sketch, these friendly creatures were so tame they would barely move out of the way of the slow-moving traffic. Probably at the peak of their seasonal molt, even the lambs looked quite scruffy up close, but their handsome lines and their sure-footed grace were much in evidence.

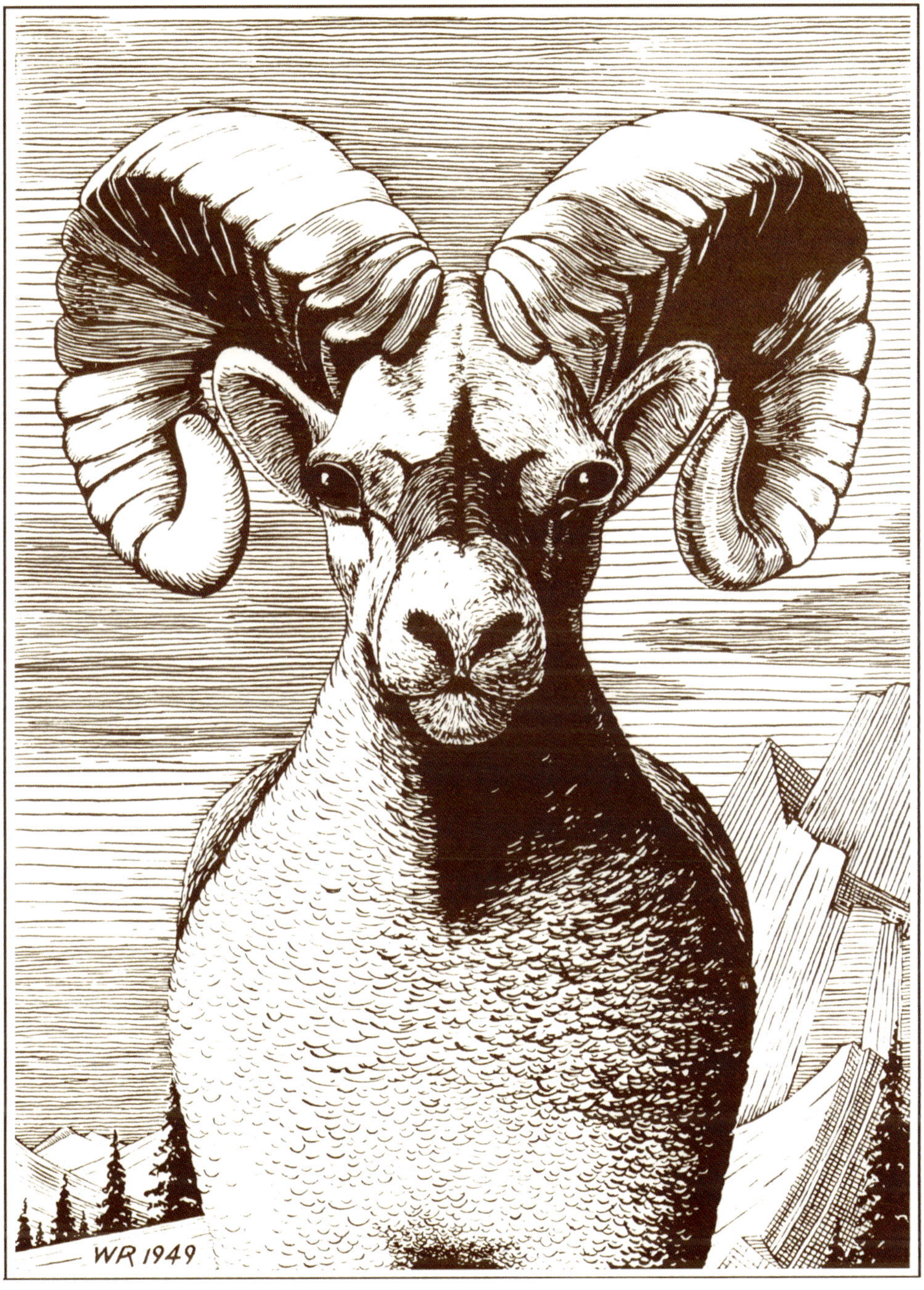
WR 1949

MARIE CREEK BACKWATER
1992

Originally painted in 1966
Oil on panel
60 x 75 cm

When we lived on Canadian Forces Base Cold Lake, we always considered Marie Creek, which meandered through the forest not far from our back door, to be one of the most appealing spots on base. In fall the rust and scarlet of the low bushes at shoreline often cast stunning reflections in the stillness of the backwater near us. In this semi-abstract painting I tried to capture the undulating rhythms of the forest, along with the symmetrical appeal of a still reflection.

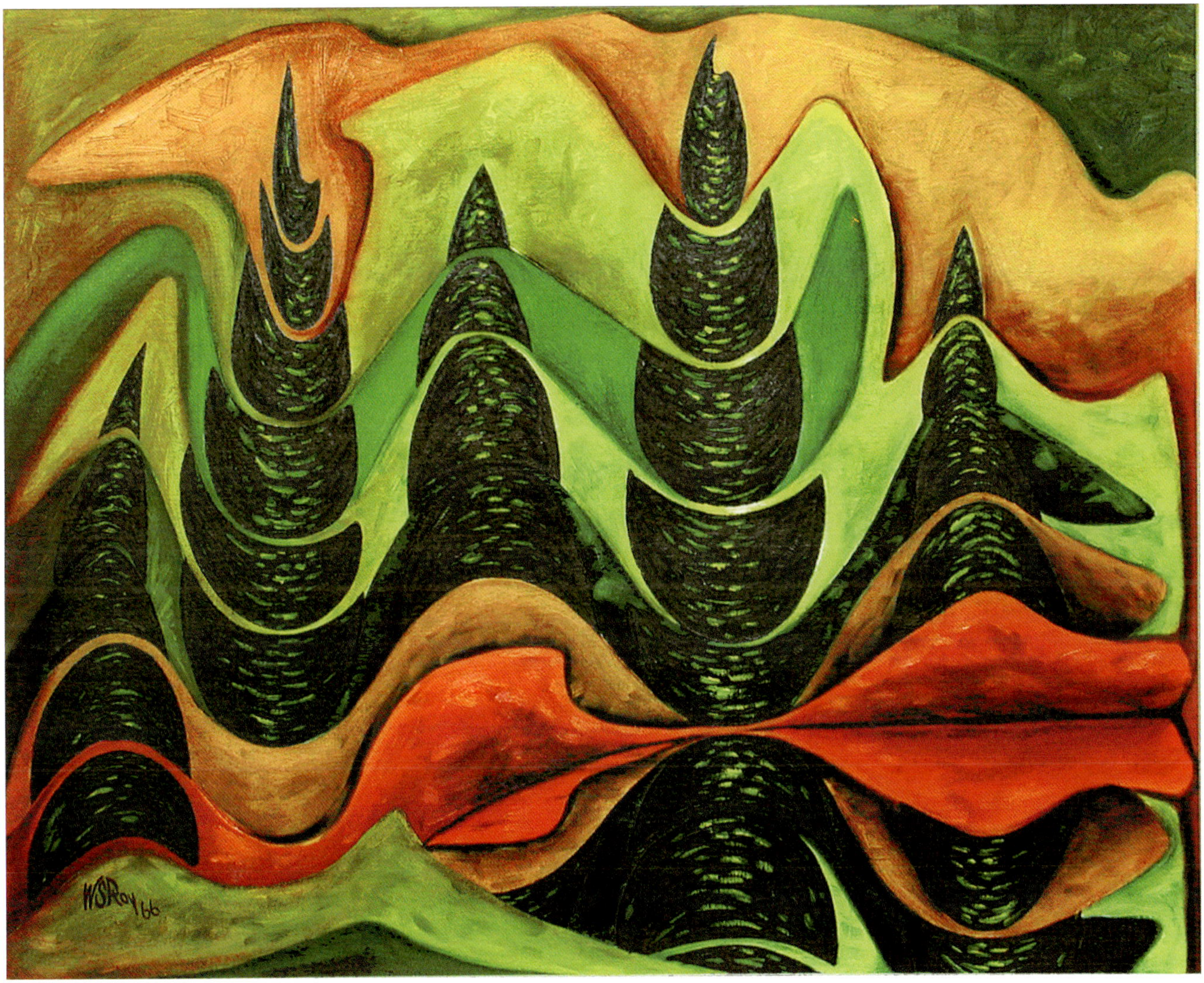
WSRoy '66

CANOLA FIELD
1993

Originally painted in 1993
Acrylic on paper
45 x 55.5 cm

In July, 1991, on the highway to Waterton National Park, Heidi and I were captivated by a spectacular view of lush canola crops near Pincher Creek. Seemingly endless, these gently undulating, starkly yellow fields stretched to the distant backdrop of foothills and the Rockies. Seeded right to the edges of several meandering dry coulees, the yellow canola stood out in sharp contrast to the dull green of the prairie grass and the deeper green of the other crops in the foreground where we stood beside the car.

A dramatic note was added for us that day by a distant, approaching thunder storm, usually a welcome source of moisture for the crops, but also a possible cause of destruction if hail were involved as it was in 1992, when most of the canola crops near Pincher Creek were wiped out.

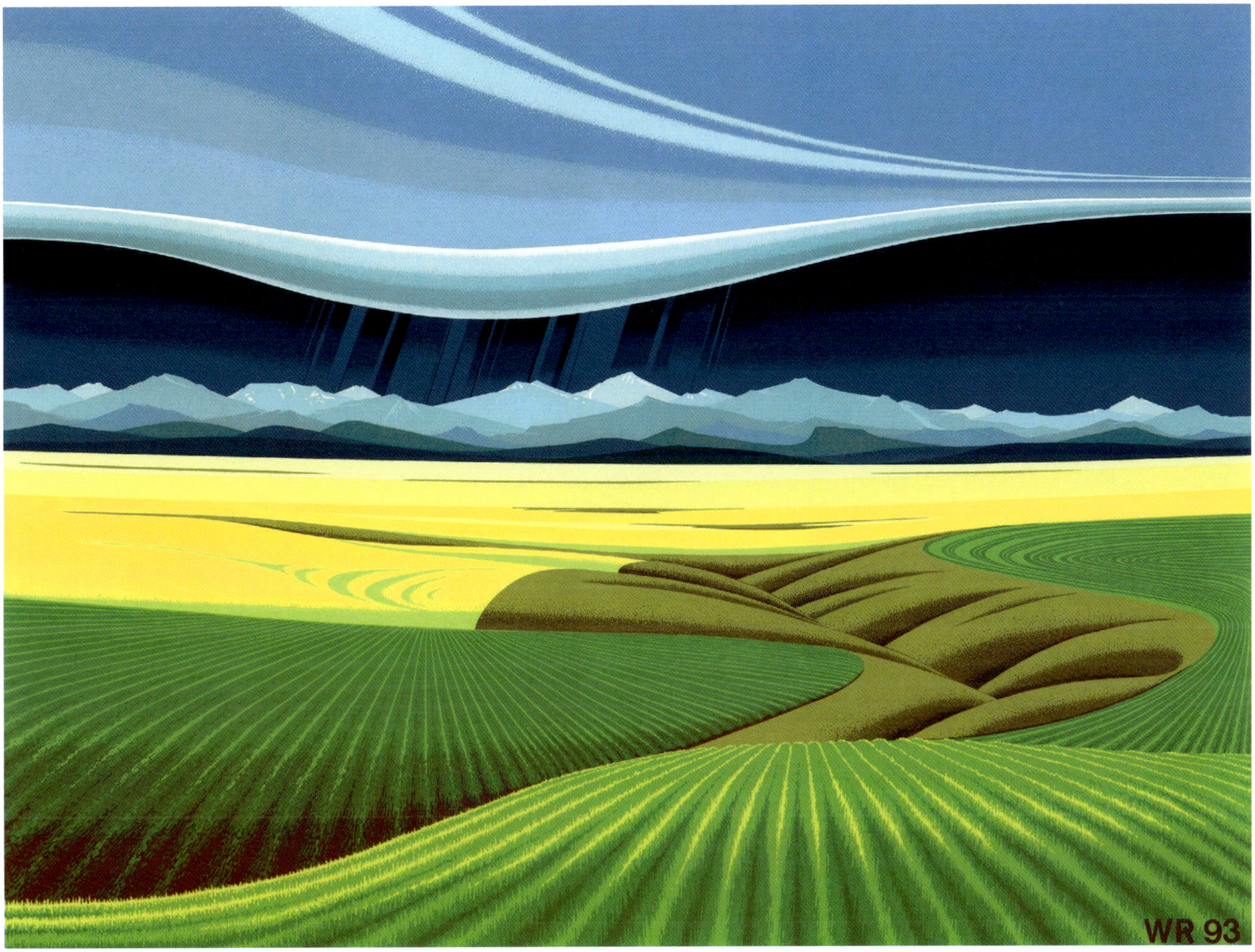
WR 93

SUNSET AT ENGLISH BAY #1
1997

Originally painted in 1967
Oil on panel
50 x 59.5 cm

This painting is the first of a series of three made from the same sketches and remembrances of English Bay, one of the most striking spots along the extensive shoreline of Cold Lake, near which we lived for many years. Along parts of the beach is a heavy stand of birch and poplar—strangely open at the bottom but densely leaved overhead. My aim was to capture how a brilliant sunset, reflected in the lake, penetrated the dense crosshatching of trunks and branches.

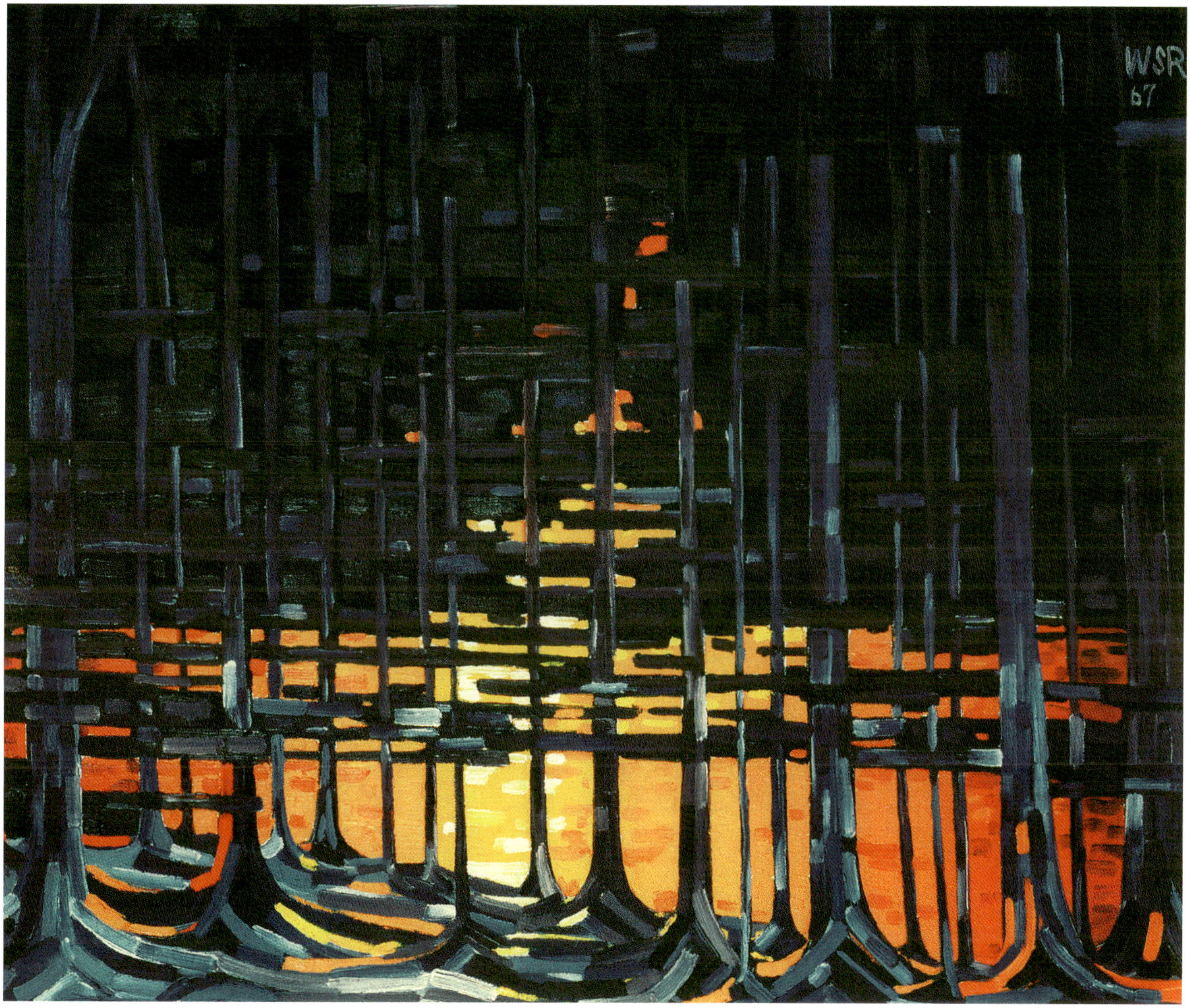
WSR
67

SUNSET AT ENGLISH BAY #2
1994

Originally painted in 1967
Oil on panel
44.5 x 60 cm

Second in the series of three English Bay paintings is this abstract study in which only the curved lines were taken from the scene, leaving the other lines of nature out of the design. The leafless tree trunks along the lakeshore are suggested by the heavy, curving upright lines. The canopy of leaves above is suggested by the thinner curved lines branching out and overlapping against the cool, indigo shadows. Details of the warm sunset reflecting off the water, visible between the tree trunks, are kept minimal—in an attempt to render only the light itself.

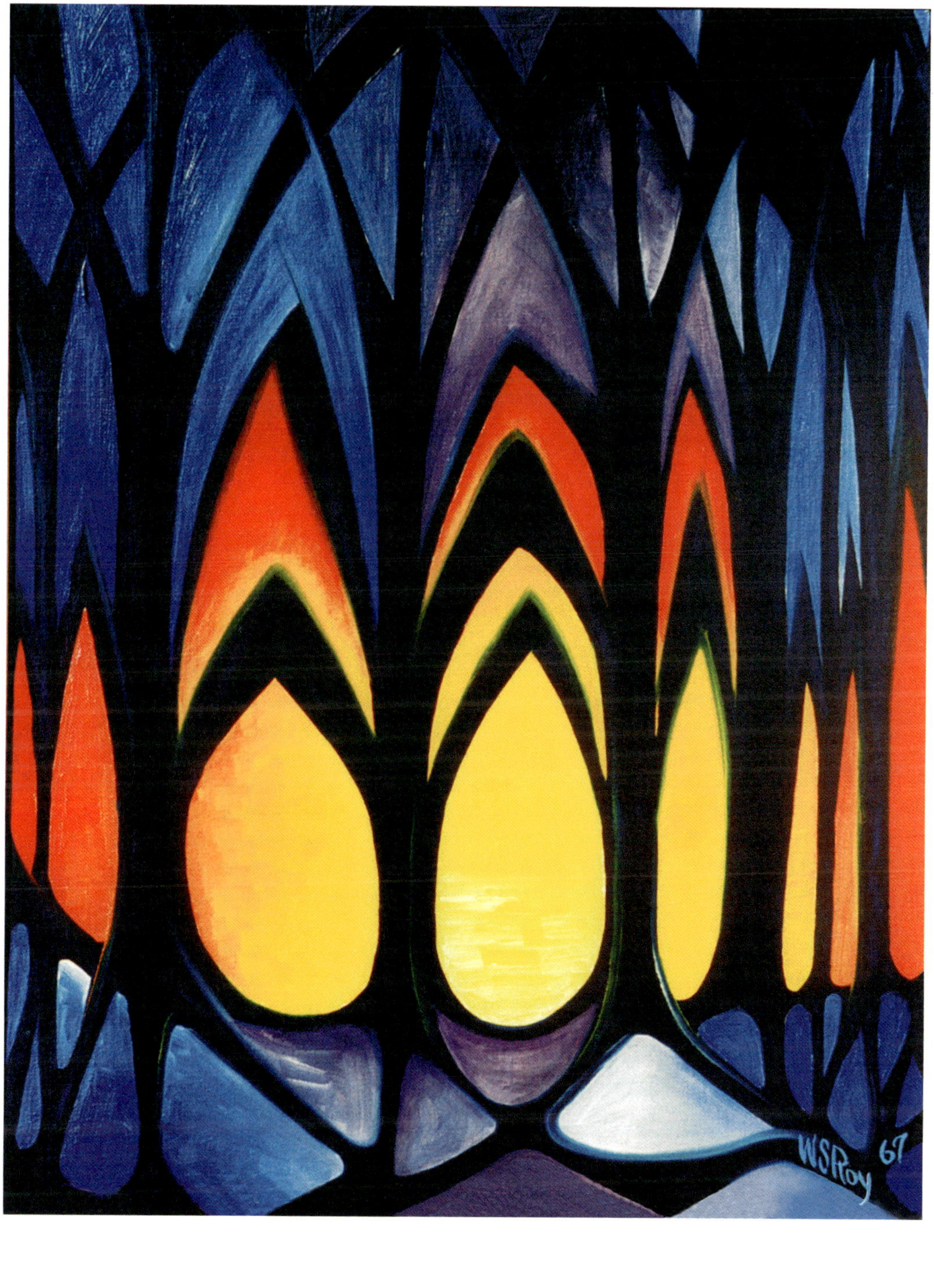
WSRoy 67

SUNSET AT ENGLISH BAY #3
1998

Originally painted in 1968
Oil on panel
60 x 75 cm

This painting, the last of the three in the English Bay series, is an abstract study which includes only straight horizontal or vertical lines. No curved or slanted lines belong in this chosen discipline. The basic palette of the original painting remains. For this abstract discipline I acknowledge my indebtedness to the Dutch painter, Piet Mondrian (1872 – 1944) who first created paintings in this manner, but who went even farther by limiting his palette to only the three primary colors.

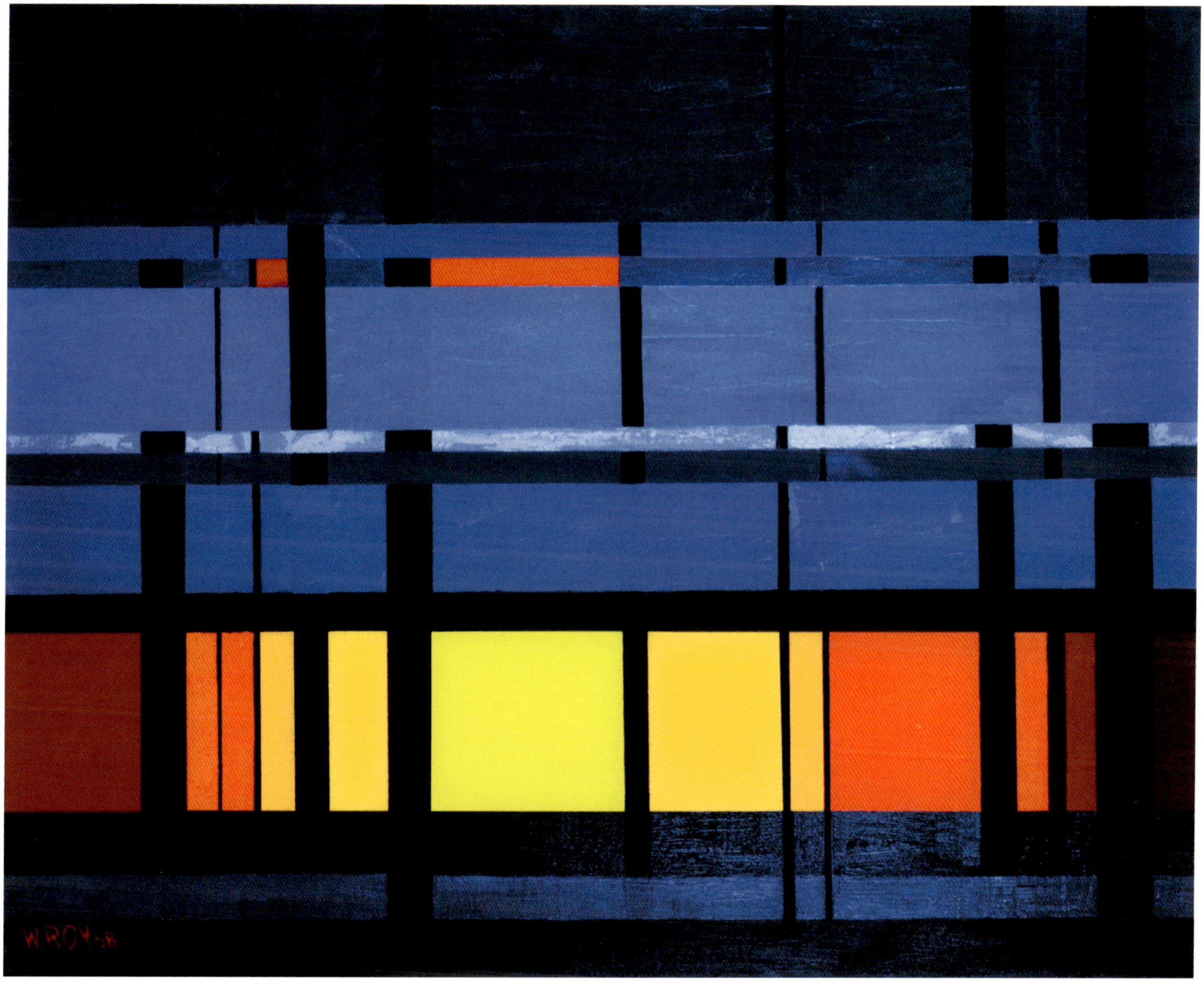

CARTHY FUGUE
1995

Originally painted in 1995
Acrylic on paper
24 x 30 cm

Shortly after moving to Calgary in the fall of 1994 we had the good fortune to attend the Calgary International Pipe Organ Festival held in October. The **Carthy Organ** in the Jack Singer Concert Hall was the principal organ of the five featured in the "crawl" (tour). This magnificent instrument stands out, in our estimation, as one of Calgary's finest assets, a truly remarkable treasure for a smaller "western" city.

In this little painting I made an admittedly fanciful attempt to portray the **sound** of the Carthy organ! Of the Carthy's 6008 pipes I have shown only 34, rearranged in an asymmetrical design.

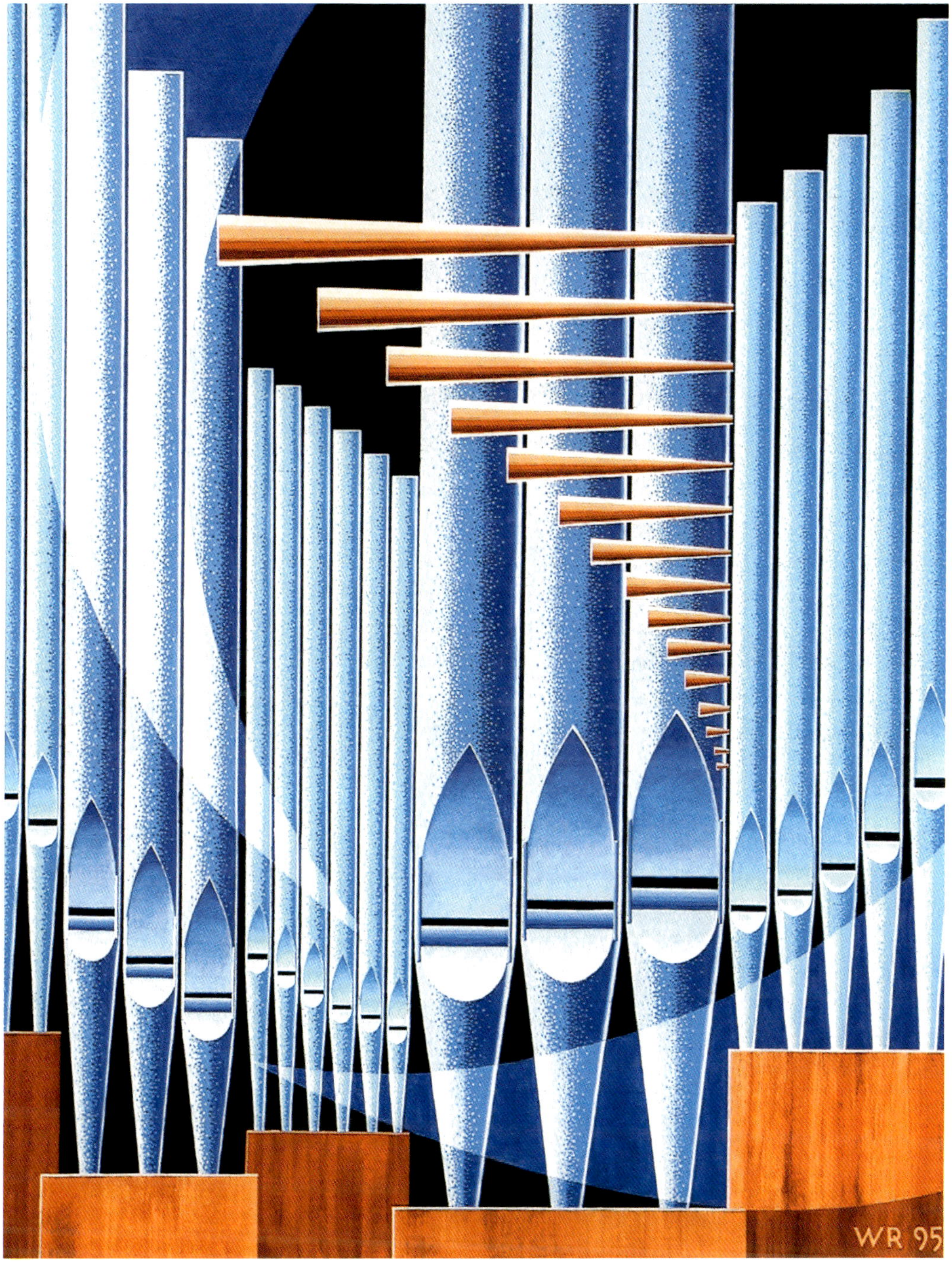
WR 95

FOREST PATTERNS
1996

Originally painted in 1966
Oil on panel
54.5 x 70 cm

In all its parts and in all its stages of growth there is nothing in nature more harmonious than a tree. In this painting, as in others before and after, I tried to show that remarkable harmony: The basic shape of a pine cone, for example, is replicated in the shape of the coniferous tree itself. In a deciduous tree the branches and root system are replicated in the vein structure of a single leaf.

It is not only a harmony of shapes but also of color—especially in fall. What could be more richly harmonious than the black-green of a spruce against the golden yellow of a poplar?

Perhaps Alfred Joyce Kilmer said it best:

> I think that I shall never see
> A poem lovely as a tree;
>
> A tree whose hungry mouth is pressed
> Against the earth's sweet flowing breast...

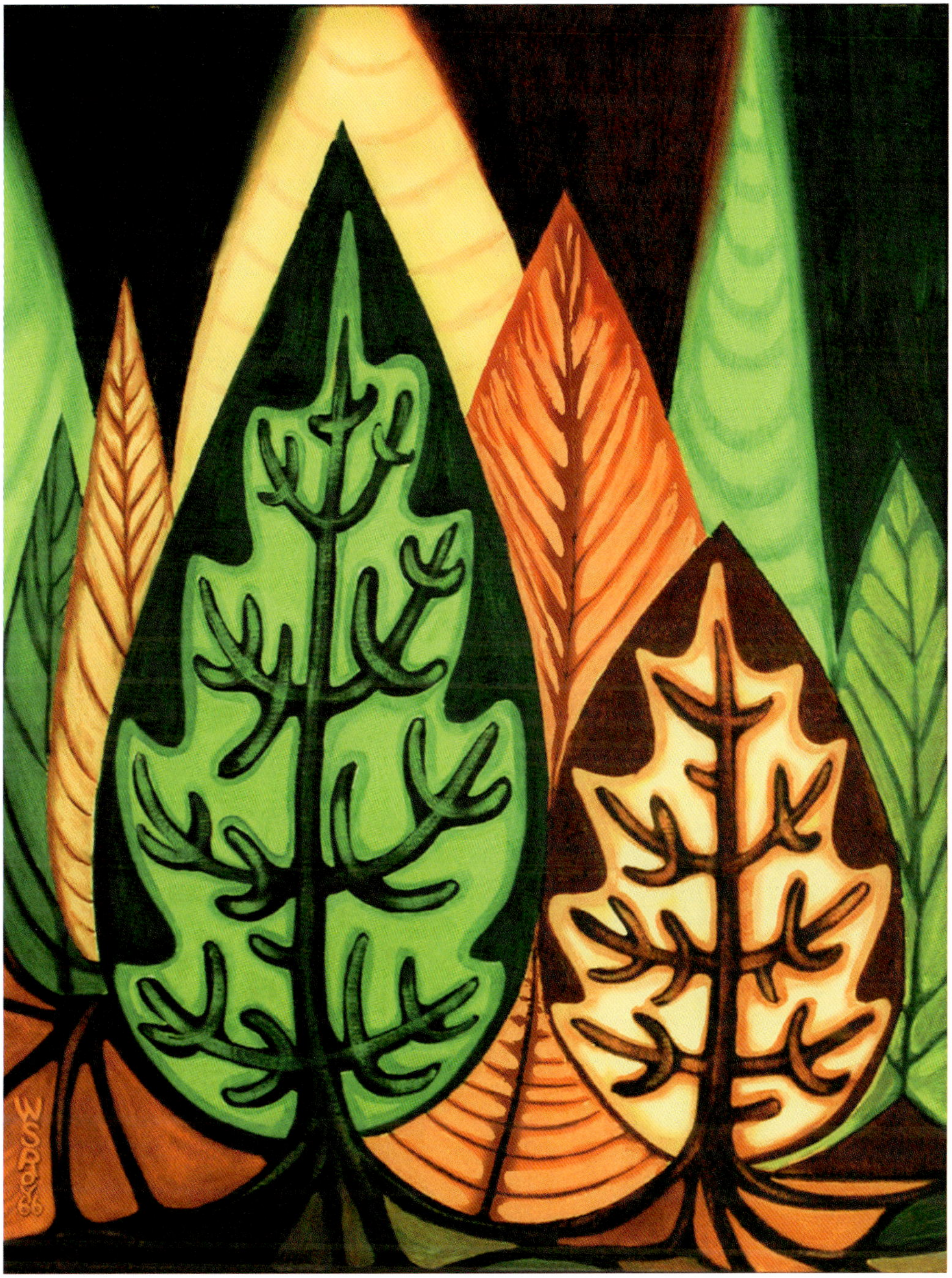

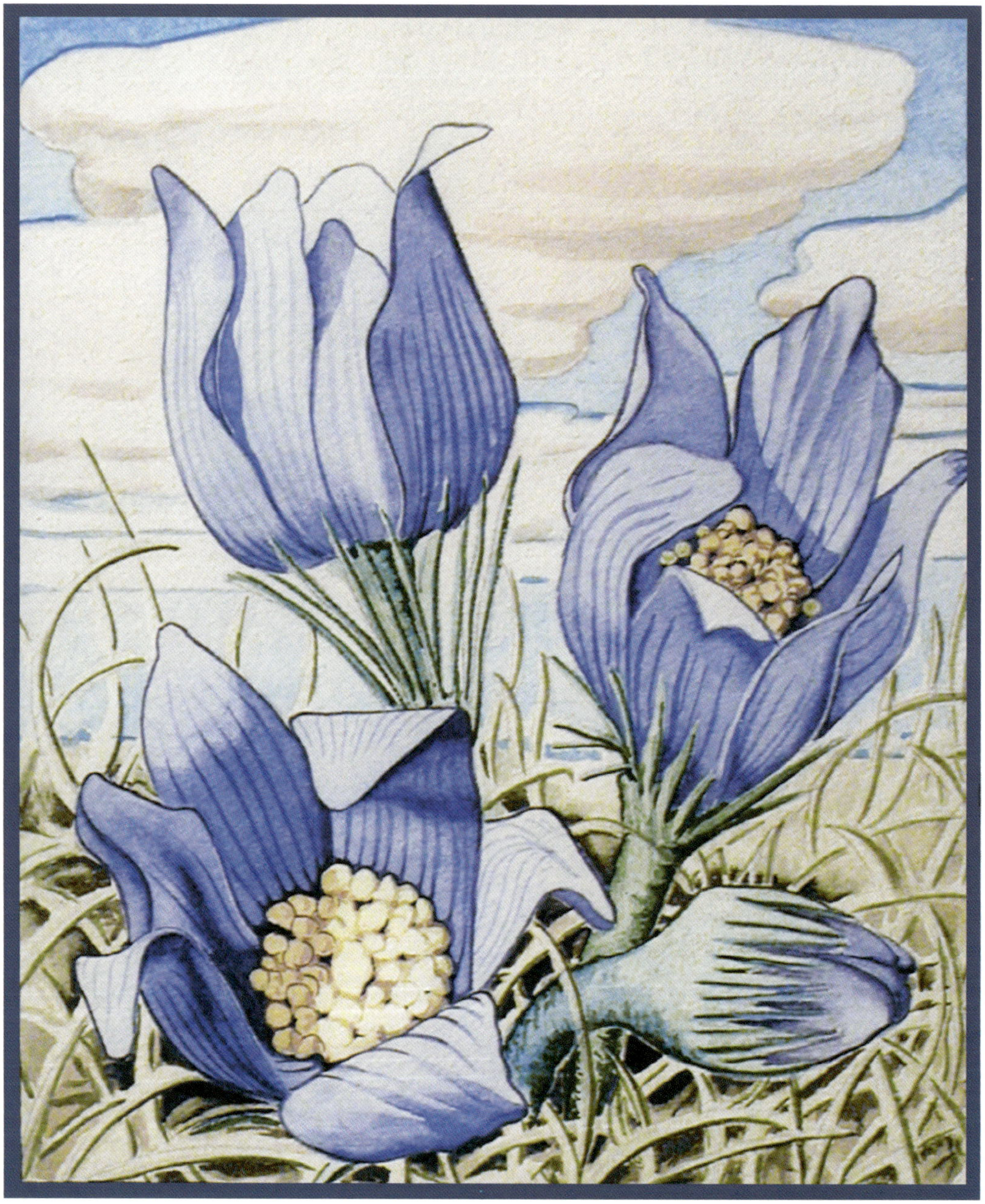

Crocuses 1949, watercolor, 17.2 x 20.5 cm

THE COMPUTER GRAPHICS CHRISTMAS CARDS

My last five Christmas cards, discussed and illustrated on pp 110 – 119, were designed on computer. Current computer graphics software is really quite versatile, but unfortunately some of the features in these programs seem to be shortcuts for harassed, overworked graphic artists with limited design and color backgrounds. These "slick" or "tricky" features—just a notch above "clip art"—produce results that are usually just "cute" but are sometimes downright *kitsch*! Designers who aspire to individuality and simplicity must, of course, avoid over-use of these few questionable features.

All told, there is much potential in present computer graphics programs. Whether it is the versatile control over the hue, value and chroma of a color; the accuracy of a vector drawing; or the easy duplication of shapes, there are few limitations for a knowledgeable artist or designer. In fact, Ernest Lindner would probably decry the lack of any real discipline which was always imposed in the traditional media such as a linocut or a watercolor painting.

Some day computer art may gain real status in the art world. In the meantime those of us who strive for a degree of harmony and unity in our work may have to set up our own limitations and visual discipline. Perhaps we could apply to computer art what Robert Frost, the great American poet, said about poetry. In discussing the difference between the highly ordered "blank verse" and "free verse", Frost said, "Writing free verse is like playing tennis with the net down." Can we say that neither art nor poetry can thrive and endure without discipline?

RICHMOND HILL
1999

This little "abstract" was my first Christmas card composed on computer. An early version of Adobe Illustrator software proved quite adequate for the task. Like *RCAF Station Cold Lake* on p 31 or *Prairie Sentinels* on p 88—both about a half-century old—this design is another attempted "geographical condensation". This time, in a light hearted way, I tried to distil into one visual statement the whole environment of Richmond Hill, our new Calgary housing area. Because of all the development around us, by the time the card was designed we could no longer see the mountains and foothills from our house—but we knew they were there! Also, you don't usually see a "Chinook arch" at night, but with artistic licence, you can get away with it.

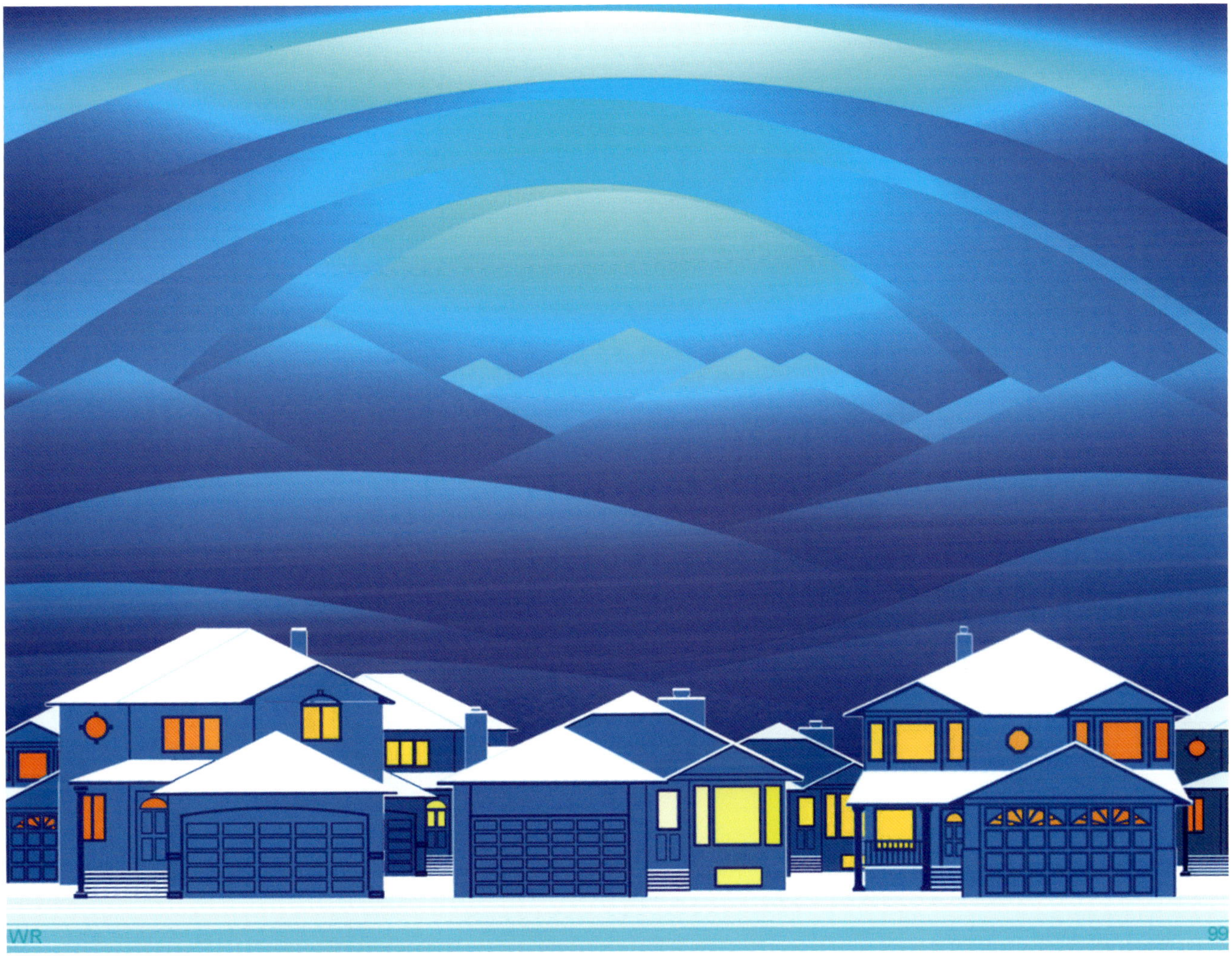
WR
99

CALGARY CITYSCAPE
2000

In this computer-designed Christmas card I attempted to show one quite noticeable change in the skyline of our rapidly growing city: The second tower of the Bankers Hall complex, shown on the left of the design, reached near completion in the year 2000.

For this card I was getting used to Corel Draw 9 which is truly versatile if less "friendly" than the Adobe software used in 1999. Although quite eye-catching, the design has a little too much going on in it. Ernest Lindner would say I needed "stricter discipline" as I explored the almost limitless potential of computer art.

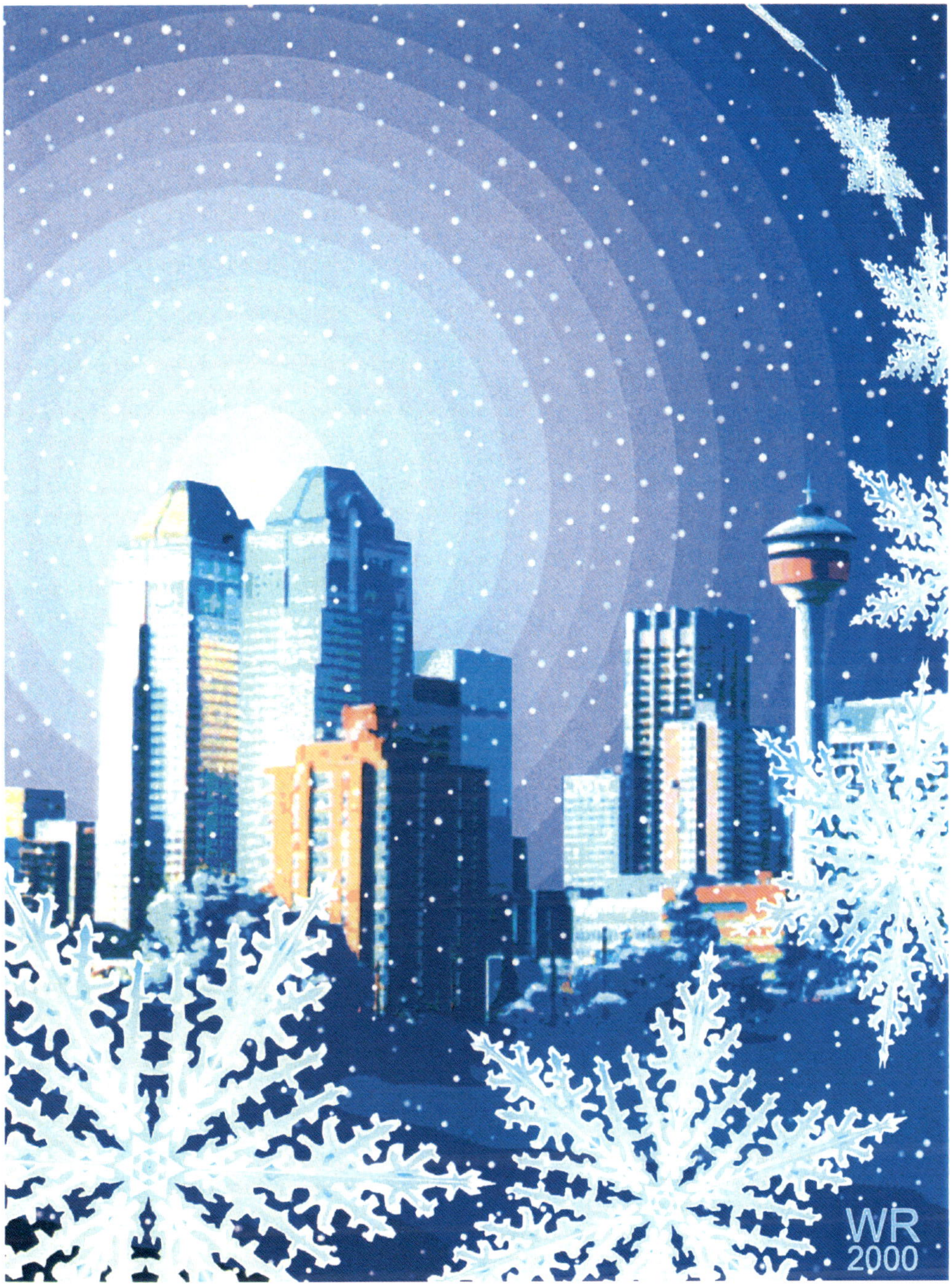
WR
2000

RIDE WITH THE WIND
2001

Sometimes politicians do get it right: On September 5, 2001, the **C-trains in Calgary** were switched over to "green power" from Vision Quest Windelectric Farm near Pincher Creek, 210 kilometres southwest of the city. By January Vision Quest expected to be operating sixty of these tall and graceful turbines, twelve of which are needed to supply the 21,000 megawatts of electricity required annually for our C-trains. At a capital cost of only $1 million for each turbine, with very low maintenance costs—and an endless free (and abundant!) supply of Alberta wind—these "windelectric" turbines make good sense.

Although not quite as efficient as space-consuming solar cells, the tiny footprint of these windmills makes them compatible with the agriculture of southern Alberta. It is estimated that the use of this "green power" costs Calgarians only about one-half cent more for each C-train fare!

Very little artistic skill is needed to portray the striking beauty of a wind farm! On our visit to Pincher Creek in August, Heidi and I were both taken with the elegant grace of these huge machines. Part of the overall visual impact is, of course, sheer size. Some of the larger Danish made "Vestas" are about thirteen storeys tall with turbine blades spanning a diameter the width of three city lots! Since the very first windmills of Europe, which came into prominence during the twelfth century, there has always been an inherent functional beauty in these machines. I tried to capture a bit of it in *Ride with the Wind.*

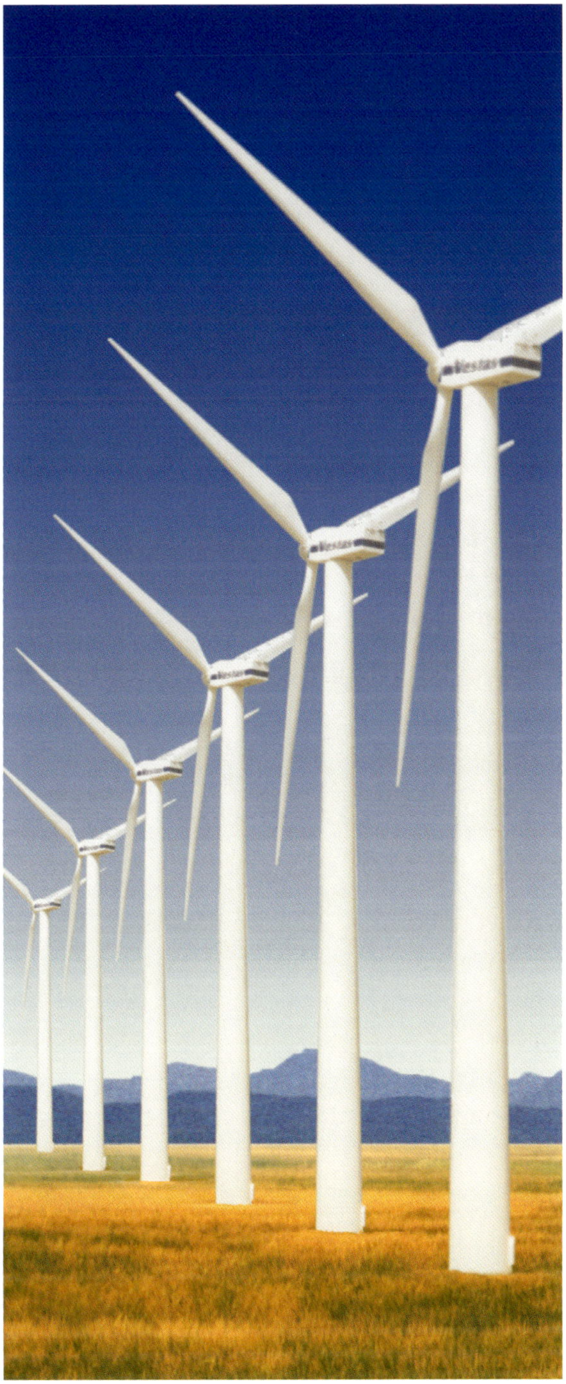
Vestas

SYMBOLS OF FAITH
2002

CHRISTIANITY
About 33% of world population is **Christian.** The main branches of the faith are Roman Catholic, Orthodox and Protestant.

ISLAM
Originating nearly 1400 years ago in Arabia and now the fastest growing religion, **Islam** is embraced by about 22% of world population. The word, **Islam**, means "peace" or "submission".

HINDUISM
Hinduism, the world's oldest living religion, dates back to at least 2000 BC. About 15% of world population is Hindu.

NONE
About 14% of world population has no formal religious belief.

BUDDHISM
About 500 years older than Christianity, this meditative faith began in India, but spread east throughout Asia. About 6% of world population is **Buddhist.**

JUDAISM
About 14 million* people embrace this historically important faith which is nearly as old as Hinduism.

TAOISM
The **Taoist** symbol is often used to represent Chinese traditional religion which includes, among others, three *basic* philosophies...**Confucianism**, **Taoism**, itself, and **Buddhism** About 225 million people follow the various tenets of this complex faith.

SIKHISM
Originating in fifteenth century northern India, this monotheistic faith is now embraced by about 23 million people.

BAHA'I
Originating in present-day Iran, and only about 150 years old, the **Baha'i** faith now has about 6 million followers. Baha'i stresses such principles as economic justice and women's rights.

JAINISM
Not as old as **Hinduism** or **Judaism**, but dating back to the 5th century BC, the peace-loving **Jainists** have about 4 million followers-- mostly in India.

SHINTOISM
Shinto, the traditional, nature revering religion of Japan, which dates back to at least 1000 BC, has about 4 million followers.

*Population figures are from Adherents.com, September, 2002

There would be much less terrorism in the world if any one of the great religions were followed with diligence and moderation. Religious *differences* do not cause wars. Religious *intolerance* and *extremism do*! We all have a healthy set of prejudices, often including an intolerance of our neighbor's religion... or *lack* thereof! Our set of prejudices may include not only religious intolerance, but also a toxic mix of economic, political, sexual and racial intolerance. Throw in corporate fraud (of the "Bre-x" or "Enron" variety) and the rampant greed for oil... Then war and terrorism are inevitable.

Similar to *World Religions,* the 1980 card on p 69, the overlapping symbols in this design are an attempt to show the harmonies and interrelationships among world religions.

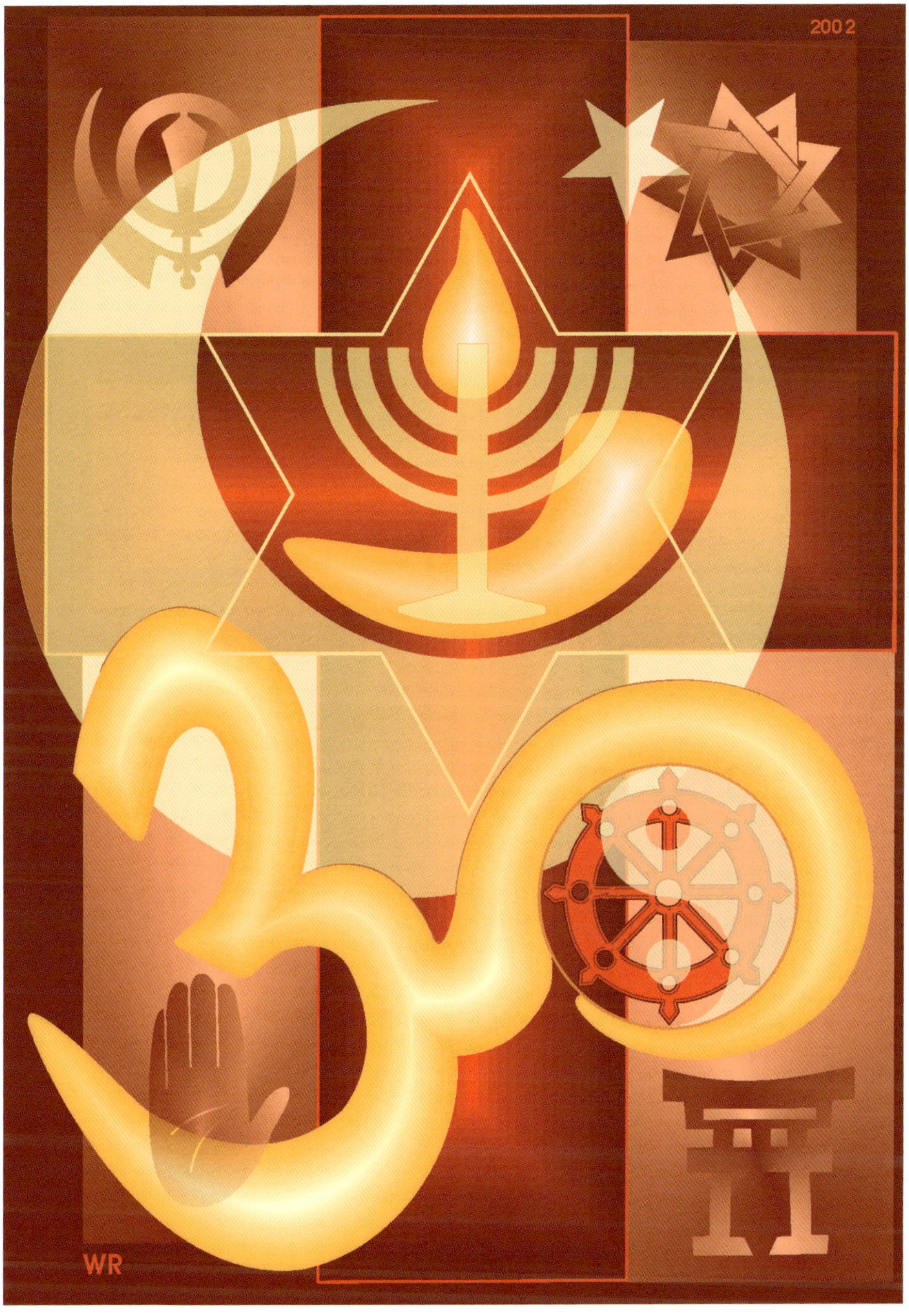
2002
WR

PHOENIX RISEN
2003

On October 15, 2002 the Calgary Philharmonic filed for bankruptcy protection and the great orchestra was silenced for over four months while it cast about for the $1.5 million required for solvency! Changes in management and financial structure promised a new solidity and permanence. Thanks to financial help from private and corporate donors, the CPO musicians themselves, and our (sometimes surprisingly astute) federal, provincial and city governments, the CPO did not die. Like the phoenix—a bird in Egyptian mythology which could consume itself by fire but rise from the ashes young and beautiful to live again—our orchestra has come back to us renewed and very much alive!

The 2003 season began on September 14 with the outdoor "Mozart-on-the-Mountain" performance in Canmore. Ignoring persistent rain showers, a record 7,300 patrons enjoyed a lively symphonic program. There was also substantial attendance at the regular concerts in the city. The resurrection of the CPO seems rock solid!

The four basic elements of this computer design—violin, French horn, trumpet and "phoenix"—were all "hand drawn" and manipulated on Corel Draw 9 and Corel Draw 12 software.

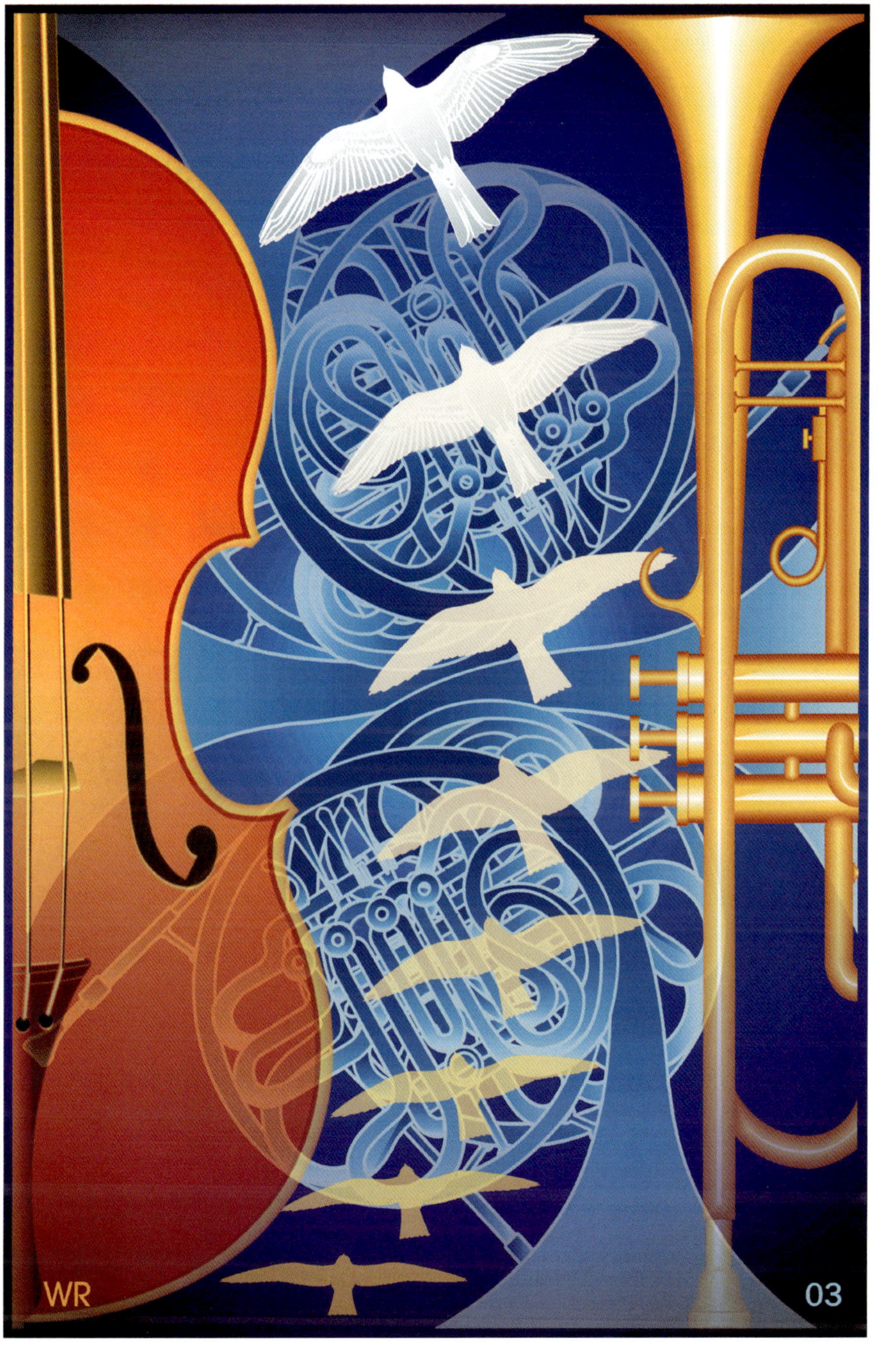
WR
03

THE 50 CHRISTMAS CARDS, A DATED SUMMARY

	YEAR	CARD TITLE	MEDIUM	PAGE
1.	1945	*Farm Home*	linocut	13
2.	1946	*Snowbound*	linocut	15
3.	1947	*Prairie Snowdrifts*	linocut	17
	1948	no card		
4.	1949	*The Mountains of Vancouver*	linocut	19
	1950	no card		
	1951	no card		
	1952	no card		
5.	1953	*Meadow Lake Grain Elevators*	linocut	21
6.	1954	*Away in a Manger*	linocut	23
7.	1955	*Christ in Christmas*	linocut	25
8.	1956	*Northern Lights*	linocut	27
9.	1957	*Woodsman*	linocut	29
	1958	no card		
	1959	no card		
	1960	no card		
10.	1961	*RCAF Station Cold Lake*	linocut	31
11.	1962	*African Madonna*	linocut	33
	1963	no card		
12.	1964	*Family Christmas*	serigraph	39
13.	1965	*Forty Below*	serigraph	41
14.	1966	*Autumn Forest*	serigraph	43
15.	1967	*Giving*	serigraph	45
16.	1968	*The Rockies*	serigraph	47
17.	1969	*Kids Dancing*	serigraph	49
18.	1970	*A Walk in the Woods*	serigraph	51
19.	1971	*Brass Band*	serigraph	53
20.	1972	*Family Silhouette*	serigraph	55
21.	1973	*Guitar Quartet*	serigraph	57

	YEAR	CARD TITLE	MEDIUM	PAGE
22.	1974	*PAX*	serigraph	59
23.	1975	*Helping Hands*	serigraph	61
24.	1976	*Prost!*	serigraph	63
25.	1977	*Northern Pine*	serigraph	65
26.	1978	*Alberta Rose*	serigraph	67
	1979	no card		
27.	1980	*World Religions*	serigraph	69
28.	1981	*Grain Elevators*	serigraph	71
29.	1982	*Candelabrum*	serigraph	73
30.	1983	*Retired!*	serigraph	75
31.	1984	*Carol of the Bells*	serigraph	77
32.	1985	*Yule Fire*	serigraph	79
33.	1986	*Stained Glass Forest*	serigraph	81
34.	1987	*Northern Lights*	serigraph	83
35.	1988	*Heavy Oil*	serigraph	85
36.	1989	*Hoarfrost*	reproduction	91
37.	1990	*Yin and Yang*	serigraph	87
38.	1991	*Rocky Mountain Sheep*	reproduction	93
39.	1992	*Marie Creek Backwater*	reproduction	95
40.	1993	*Canola Field*	reproduction	97
41.	1994	*Sunset at English Bay #2*	reproduction	101
42.	1995	*Carthy Fugue*	reproduction	105
43.	1996	*Forest Patterns*	reproduction	107
44.	1997	*Sunset at English Bay #1*	reproduction	99
45.	1998	*Sunset at English Bay #3*	reproduction	103
46.	1999	*Richmond Hill*	computer graphic	111
47.	2000	*Calgary Cityscape*	computer graphic	113
48.	2001	*Ride with the Wind*	computer graphic	115
49.	2002	*Symbols of Faith*	computer graphic	117
50.	2003	*Phoenix Risen*	computer graphic	119

ACKNOWLEDGEMENTS

My wife, Heidi, and my brother, Frank, both have a lively interest in the chronology of events touching the lives of friends and family. Also, they are both patient and capable organizers. As indicated in my dedication, Heidi's constant help and encouragement promoted continuity in my "Sunday painting" endeavors. Also, it was mostly Heidi's enthusiasm and organizational help that inspired my decision to produce this little book about our Christmas cards and the lives and times of the people involved. Thank you, Heidi.

Several years ago, quite on his own initiative, Frank decided to list, date and provide descriptive names for all of my Christmas cards. Although Frank's interest in my work was always a constant, this unexpected chronological list was really the germ of our decision to consider the hard work of producing a book. I thank Frank not only for the inspiration, but also for his constructive criticism of the manuscript and the proofreading that he and Heidi undertook on my behalf.

Warren Roy
Calgary